PERSONAL GROWTH

IN THE
MULTI-DIMENSIONAL
MULTIVERSE

FRANK MARCELLO ANTONETTI

BALBOA.PRESS
A DIVISION OF HAY HOUSE

Balboa Press books may be ordered through booksellers or by contacting:

Balboa Press
A Division of Hay House
1663 Liberty Drive
Bloomington, IN 47403
www.balboapress.com
844-682-1282

Because of the dynamic nature of the Internet, any web addresses or links contained in this book may have changed since publication and may no longer be valid. The views expressed in this work are solely those of the author and do not necessarily reflect the views of the publisher, and the publisher hereby disclaims any responsibility for them.

The author of this book does not dispense medical advice or prescribe the use of any technique as a form of treatment for physical, emotional, or medical problems without the advice of a physician, either directly or indirectly. The intent of the author is only to offer information of a general nature to help you in your quest for emotional and spiritual well-being. In the event you use any of the information in this book for yourself, which is your constitutional right, the author and the publisher assume no responsibility for your actions.

Any people depicted in stock imagery provided by Getty Images are models, and such images are being used for illustrative purposes only.
Certain stock imagery © Getty Images.

Print information available on the last page.

ISBN: 978-1-9822-7776-5 (sc)
ISBN: 978-1-9822-7777-2 (e)

Library of Congress Control Number: 2021924028

Balboa Press rev. date: 12/06/2021

Contents

Dedication

I dedicate this book to the many modern philosophers who came before me, such as: Hugh Everett III, who wrote and lectured on his – *Many worlds theory*. 1950s, Max Planck, Albert Einstein, Niels Bohr, Richard Feynman, Werner Heisenberg, Erwin Schrodinger who all contributed to our modern-day study of Quantum Physics. Helena Petrovna Blavatsky – Theosophy, Mary Baker, Eddie – Christian Science, and Edgar Cayce - A.R.E who were by the mid-1800s to set the groundwork for the Metaphysics of today. Lastly, I mention the many Greek Philosophers that inspired me:

- Epicurus (c. 341-270 BCE)
- Anaxagoras (c. 500-428 BCE)
- Pythagoras (c. 570-495 BCE)
- Heraclitus (c. 535-475 BCE)
- Democritus (c. 460-370 BCE)
- Empedocles (c. 490-330 BCE)
- Thales (c. 624-546 BCE)
- Aristotle (c. 384-322 BCE)

Preface

I wrote this book as a sequel to my last book – The Enigma of God, a revelation to man - Balboa press 2012, to modernize the public to new insights in the field of quantum physics include personal growth both on a spirit and soul levels. My first book was more of a spiritual encouragement self-help book. I felt that I channel its material from a particularly advanced soul somewhere. My current book is not channeled automatic writing was employed. I used the metaphysical principles of each atom in me that holds a reflection to all reality. I thus channeled my inner awareness to write this book. I have learned over time that channeling material from an external source may have filthy consequences, and manipulation of those sources. My last book's material is wholesome, and its source is advanced but unschooled in dealing with humans and their help needed in their personal lives. I encourage my public to read my last book after this current one; its overall glow is beneficial and its reviews to be of self-growth.

I feel that I am qualified to write this book based on quantum physics, due to my advanced personal studies in "higher math to quantum". Odd enough to say, trigonometry is the basis of all higher math, including quantum. Trig identities are needed to memorize and are essential; they should not be overlooked in our quantum math preparations. Advanced algebra and geometry are required too. Between the two, we can take up pre-calculus, then calculus one for two-dimensional graphing, then calculus two or physics, then calculus three for three-Dimensional shapes inter- reactions. However, the above is not needed to understand my material. Though, the proofing of my findings would need such higher math skills, though.

I have viewed many YouTube videos and found many to be of sound logic. I have disagreed with a lot of their findings, as well. I have considered them all to be superficial and lacking the elements of personal growth both on a soul and spirit levels.

This is the reason; I wrote this book. It was written in 2021 and end year for final self-editing. This current book is my first book not using a proofreader/rewriter. I spent 3.4k on editing serves for my first book and decided not to spend that money again. My English writings were uneducated in 2011 and not ready to self-editing The Enigma of God. My writing is currently – first-year college. This book is self-edited, which is uncommon to see in the literal world.

I also feel qualified to write on this material due to my twelve years of training at the Theosophy Hall in NYC – The United Hall of Theosophy, and studies in the Christian Science, and Mormon's religions. My general alternative spiritual education is evident in my first book. Alternative Spirituality education is needed to write on personal growth concerning quantum physics.

I am also a gifted psychic who has worked many phones psychic lines in my past. My callbacks clients confirm my skills to be accurate. I read the Runestones, Tarot, Astrology, and Numerology; I am most gifted in automatic writings, though. I have been practicing automatic writing the longest. The skill involves placing a pen in one's hand on the paper and allowing one's pen to spell words that may seem foreign to our Minds. For my two books to date, I perform this skill with the keyboard of my laptop. I only pick up my pen to paper if my fingers fail me at my keyboard to know the unknown mysteries needed. When I do pick up the pen to paper, a rush of words flows into my Mind. I would quickly notate them to typing on my laptop to preserve them.

This book is not considered channeled as seen in many books in the New Aged movements. My first book – the Enigma of God was channeled. This book uses another style of inspiration writings – not a New Aged style of writings. I feel that my current book is written on a much higher level than most New Aged books including my last one. I do encourage my public to read it, though. For an inspiring New Aged book- it is encouraging! May we please use reflection in reading this current book – Personal growth in the multi-dimensional multiverse? There will be many abstract thoughts that would need inner reflections.

Introduction

The book is based on intuitive research in Multi-Dimension, Multiverse studies. What can you do with this book answers the following question? Do you want to amaze all your friends at cocktail parties with knowledge about the Golden age of math? Would you like an introduction to quantum and astrophysics physics for personal growth? Do you want to know how modern insights in the multi-Dimensional Multiverse and beyond involve you as an individual? Do you want to be – Hip on the current banter of contemporary science? Do you like to be considered as – Today's man/woman accredited with having erudite conversations? If you can answer Yes to all these questions – then read on!!!

The Golden Age of Math has gone beyond what the New Agers, Hindu Philosophies, and Eastern Philosophies can offer. This new math had left them all in the dust. Only Theosophy which is the literary works of Helena Petrovna Blavatsky has insights like those I write. Mrs. Blavatsky wrote about spiritual growth in our wheel of the Third Dimension. She also wrote about the state of Pralaya – a rest. In such Pralaya, a Universe closed in on itself and died. When needed, it can regrow but in a new and differently unique manner. I have written about such Pralaya in my Chapter of the Ninth to Twelfth Dimensions. Yes, Theosophy has greatly enriched my knowledge in the spiritual fields I possess.

For those unfamiliar with Blavatsky's literary works, I recommend it to broaden your knowledge. Both Blavatsky of Theosophy and Mary Baker Eddie, founder of the Christian Scientists faith, is the foundation of our modern New Aged movement. Oddly enough, their time was in the middle of the 1800s, and the New Agers started in the Mid 70s. The Christian Scientists' faith is too often confused with Scientology, founded by L. Ron Hubbard in December of 1953 in Southern California. I will educate us in knowing how the two are separate. Scientology teaches that each human has a reactive Mind that responds to life's traumas, clouding the analytic Mind and keeping us from experiencing reality. Their objective is to clear the Mind of negativity and open it up to clarity, fostering happiness and success. The Christian Scientists teach that prayer to the Holiness of God will heal all matters. Both faiths focus on the Mind as the director, and changing it brings healing and success. The New Aged book – A Course in Miracle teaches the same and is a plagiary of Christian Science.

Unfortunately, the New Aged Movement is not as widely spoken about compared to only twenty years ago. The internet has narrowed the public book-buying scope to individual searches on topics only. People rarely read books anymore. However, the insights in the Golden Age of Math have reawakened higher Mind studies again. This time to a much deeper and vast level of abstract knowledge. I now invite you all to join the modern intelligentsia by reading the current book you have at hand.

Multi souls, spirit and life on different Dimensions will be covered with new math using negative numbers based on Gödel's theory of numbers. Gödel was very basic and skilled with insightful knowledge. I feel that my number theory is a continuation of His works, but far more complete.

The book also covers us being a full blow Third Dimension individual and living our lives to its fullest with no shame – be rich and famous! It's fine to be a full-blown ego here in our reality- yes! So, talk about my insights and make it more fashionable for friends and your cocktail party.

Lastly, I care to mention my writing style. I use my own sense of capitalizations for - ex: The Third Dimension, Thought Adjuster, Master Spirit and Realms as I feel in my book as they are proper nouns to me. I have found online editing sites helpful, but I need to stick to my writing style and not take all their suggestions to heart. The ideas made evident in this book come before and writing rules I felt when writing this book. The reason why I do not use credited to other sources as foot notes in this book is due to the nature of its writings – it is an original intuitively written book using automatic writing. I did do research in Wiki and You Tube, though. They are my only two sources to footnote. Wiki consist of borrowed material so to use that does not break any copy right laws. All wiki material has been paraphrased into my own writing style. For the most part. This book is ninety-five percent original material. I have posted You Tube videos jus to have my material borrowed and interpreted in a different style of speech for their videos.

I ask you to recommend my material to friends or pass this book on after a good read. The call to action is the growth of the common person's understanding of modern science. This book is a blend of modern science and personal spirituality grown on multiple realities. The meaning of life and true love is also covered in this book. The self-help aspect is covered in the third chapter in understanding our Dimensions needs for us and its growth. I wish you all a good read now.

Frank Marcello Antonetti

Chapter 1

The History on the Multiverse theory with an introduction to Dimensions One to Nine

D uring a public lecture, Erwin Rudolf Josef Alexander Schrödinger, a Physicist in 1952, in Dublin, Ireland, mentioned his hypothetical experiment, known today as the "Schrodinger's cat theory" in 1935, indicated multiple Histories of one event could be possible; and it happens concurrently. The hypothetical experiment states that a cat can be dead and alive at the same time if exposed to uranium. From his stimuli on the matter, the recent physicist Hugh Everette first proposed the *"many worlds,"* or the *Multiverse*, in 1957 in his doctoral thesis at Princeton University. His many worlds of Universes in multiple Dimensions may also say the *"relative state formulation"* or *"the Everett interpretation."*

Later, in Theoretical Physics, Bryce DeWitt popularized the formulation and named it *many-worlds* in the 1960s and 1970s. Though, the first mention of alternative realities was by a Greek Platonian Philosopher, *Epicurus* (341–270 BC), in His writings about His *different world's theory*; in that world are born, die and are then renewed again. He was referring to alternative realities in his essay in His old Greek manner of speaking. Epicurus developed an unsparingly materialistic metaphysics, empiricist epistemology, and hedonistic ethics of His day. Epicurus was the first to mention Atoms as the fundamental most miniature bases of all life and cannot break down further. He taught his public not to fear the Greek gods, but to live a life of self-servicing pleasure without fear of death or punishments.

In the Copenhagen interpretation of quantum mechanics, the Physicist Niels Bohr in 1929 tells us: Observation collapses a probability wave into a single definitive outcome. However, this is just one interpretation of quantum mechanics. The *many-worlds theory* proposes that the wavefunction never actually collapses. The observer follows one of those many possible paths leading to its present reality while the other paths remain independent of the observer. Each of these paths, branches off into an entirely different reality. In this episode, Niels Bohr discusses the details of the many worlds' theory and why it is not so far-fetched to think that our reality is simply one of an infinite number of realities existing beyond our notice.

In the double-slit scenario, energy particles project through the two slits. They fan out, for the most part, into roughly seven impressions. The heaviest is in the center and gets lighter to each side of the central area of impressions. In my thesis, the Second Dimension is the double-slit that project to the other four Dimensions. The First-Dimension projects directly to the Second and in turn to the Third, then the Fifth to its left, and the Fourth and Sixth to its right. The Five Dimensions all seem to project to the Seventh Dimension in turn as one beam. The Second Dimension's theme is individuality so, such intentions project to all four Dimensions for personal growth.

Schrodinger's cat animation on YouTube shows in superposition that the cat in the box can be both alive and dead simultaneously. In the hypothetical experiment, a cat is lying in a sealed container with a radioactive sample, a Geiger counter, and a bottle of poison. If the Geiger counter detects that the radioactive material has decayed, it will trigger the smashing of the bottle of poison, and the cat will die. The experiment illustrates the *Copenhagen interpretation* of quantum mechanics flaws, which states that a particle exists in all states at once *until observed.* Suppose the Copenhagen interpretation suggests the radioactive material can have simultaneously decayed and not decayed in the sealed environment. In that case, it follows the cat too is both alive and dead until the box opens.

So, the Copenhagen interpretation of quantum mechanics may have arbitrary Dimensions showing both Yes and No to any position given; this agrees with my theory that anything that exists must not exist to exist. Schrodinger's cat animation shows that alternative realities bases on the true logic of existing from a non-existing state. We call a Dimension only a point of a direction orthogonal to its lower one and its highest one. The Fourth Dimension contains up/ down, left/ right, and forward/back with the new introduction point of the directions of inside/outside. The auxiliary point of the Fifth Dimension is you/me.

The Sixth Dimension additional point is singular/multiple. We have multiple souls that do not seem to exist to each other in the Sixth Dimension as they project to lower Dimensions. Each of those Souls branching from the Sixth has different growth paths unknown to each other until the Seventh Dimension we reach. The multi-Dimensions and their multiverses allied are not all physical. They are couples in pairs as in the First and Second Dimension is energetic/dynamic. The Third Dimension is physical/stagnate, and Fourth Dimension is semi-physical/energetic. The fifth and Sixth Dimensions are energetic, with the Seventh is being neither of the two, but an indescribable element we call spirit/etheric.

The energetic Dimensions are theoretically real and subject to one's projections; it resembles an astral plane reality -self-responsive delusive energy semi- physical- but with more stable and reliable laws of advanced physics for growth. The physical Dimensions consist of a collected agreement of reality conjoin under the laws of cause and effect. The laws of Energetic Dimensions are based on the imaginative value of possibilities – I and p of calculus during the Physical the X as a value.

3

The Third, Fourth, and Seventh Dimensions are the only character-building Dimensions for public recognition and self-recognition. The Second and Sixth Dimension is semi-physical designed for planning other realities, leaving the First and Fifth to be Theoretical/Energetic and seen as politically identified for one orientation. This semi-physical Dimension forms the basis of their higher Dimensional achievements; they are projector Dimensions but physical enough to lose the use of the law of cause and effect.

The Eight Dimension is the last place where any class of physical or semi-physical matter is visible. This Dimension has a semi-physical/semi energetic to the point to balance between the two and is a real tough to describe. It is energetic, but behaves like the physical, while the Sixth and Second physically behave energetically. The Ninth Dimension is entirely Energetic but still under the law of cause and effect. The Ninth Dimension is where one can say – the governor of all karmic laws and giver of good rewards and bad punishments.

No other alternative spirituality book author has written before me regarding my original source material describing the Sixth Dimension. We have multiple souls and the Eight Dimension multiple spirits. Our perfected soul is in the Seventh, and our perfect spirit is in the Ninth Dimension of blessings or punishments.

The First Dimension reflects off from the Eighth Dimension with its riddle of the finite/infinity that only art and music can depict and comprehend. The two Dimensions dictate our joys in our lives, such as music, art; unique self-pleasures, personally unique studies; and, it has something to do with what humans call love. This type of love can be best understood in the model of body types we call humans, especially on Earth. We all should be glad to be human, I must say. I have read of angelic beings who are jealous of our possible growth as humans – they refuse to help us as angelic servants due to their jealousy of our destined growth beyond them. We design to be eventually higher than them in time.

Chapter 2

Modern insights on Christianity

The Flavian dynasty: Vespasian 69 – 79 AD, Titus 79 to 81 A.D, and Domitian 81 – 96, had their many attempts to pacify and control the rebellious Jews in a Provence called Palestine. The Roman Emperor, Titus had tried many approaches before using literature. Titus and His successors employed a scribe to write Jewish synagogues propaganda to calm that Roman state. This scribe was a Romanized Jewish priest, scholar, and Historian - Yosef Ben Matityahu (born AD 37/38, Jerusalem—died AD 100, Rome). Under His given name, Flavius Josephus, Yosef wrote many fictional scrolls on lambskin to distribute to the Jewish synagogues in Palestine to illuminate the heart of the Jews to peace and love in order to encourage educated behavior. Josephus wrote *in the guise* of a fictitious of followers of a mythical Messiah called *Yehoshua Bar Yosef*, commonly known as Jesus in the Christian Bible.

The writer Josephus and the emperors of Rome put in motion what would turn out to be the Catholic Church, unknown to them. The original intention of the Roman Caesars was to pacify the Jewish inhabitance of the Roman state of Palestine, resulting in the Jews stopping rebelling against Rome. From 66 – 70, the Roman and Israeli War engaged against that Jewish Roman providence killed many Jews out of impatience; and in 130AD, Rome scattered its people amongst the lands of the Roman Empire to finally eradicate the state of Israel. The Jews were scattered in Italy, Egypt, Asia Minor, Syria, Arabia, Greek, Ethiopia, and Spain. The fifty years of Rome using Jewish religious literature were not successful in stopping the Jewish rebellions. Still, it planted the seed for a new cult that would dominate the Roman Empire in a few hundred years.

These writings centered around a fabled *Jesus,* inspired by the Persian God Mithras and Dionysus to create a new cult that the scattered Jews brought with them. As the new faith grow, wealthy Romans became bishops, cardinals, etc., to keep the nation in control and power in that new faith. Greece, Italy, Asia Minor, and Egypt were the first to cultivate with the new cult focused on Jesus. The title of the Christ is of Greek origin as the Christos - righteous, virtuous, moral man, practical man, a good man and was first seen in writings in year 200 A.D. The images of a Jesus with long hair and a bear originated in 300 A.D in the Eastern Church and officiated in the year 600 A.D.

Regarding the Jewish Historian Josephus, his Jewish family name Matityahu – as the Biblical writer – Matthew. He used this *pen name* to write the first book of the Bible - *Matthew.* The concept of *"turn the other cheek"* is misunderstood for being a passive victim. The fact is, it means to overlook pettiness as stupidity and to rise above it. Such victim-like self-abuse is against Eastern Philosophy. If a Buddhist priest was murdered in the East, Karate fighting priests must avenge Him to avoid future life complications of revenge. Even the Old Testament writes about – an eye for an eye. The Amish people of Pennsylvania, Ohia, and New York State all misunderstood the written words of Josephus inspired by the first Century A.D mystical Essene named -Yehoshua Bar Yosef.

Many scholars have tried to educate the Jews on Greek thinking, which explains the many foreign influences on the Jews in those days. Philius Judeas - Philo was the first Jewish literary scholar who tried to educate the rebellious Jews of Palestine to a compatible Hellenistic faith. He worked with Aristobulus of Alexandria and Herod. Herod was a local King of Palestine appointed by Rome. They tried to encourage the adoration of Greek deities to the Jew's Minds set and to a more Roman/Greek manner of thinking. They only succeeded in inspiring the Jews' curiosities' casual fannies, but no dedication in Greek or any other foreign worship; they remained Jewish to the Emperor's dismay. However, many Jewish rabbis were educated in those Greek philosophies concepts and their Minds did expand. Alexander the Great conquered Israel with building many Greek temples but they were attended by a few curious. Added to the list were the local Syrian and Persian deity worship. The Zoroastrian faith had a very big influence on Israel from its very conception. Zoroastrianism was the faith of the Persian empire. Zoroastrianism is monotheistic and believed in the forces of good and bad. Israel was influenced by both Zoroastrianism and the monotheistic worship of the Egyptian Aten during the Jews captivity in Egypt. The myth of Mithras was well known and loved in Israel for hundreds of years by many communities of Jews. Yes, there were converts to pagan worship then, but it was minimal and accepted in the Jewish culture in those days. Josephus wrote about not using pagan temple prostitute as it supplied money to run the pagan temples. There was no moral statement in His writings – only a financial one.

I will now explain how foreign religious influence entered Israel. At the death of Alexander, the great, southern Syrian, Palestine, and Egypt were inherited by one of His four generals - Cassandrea, Ptolemy, Antigonus, and Seleucus. Israel was in the kingdom of Antigonosa in governing and collect taxes from them until the Seleucid Empire in 281 B.C. took over. It was founded by Seleucus I Nicator following the division of the Macedonian Empire established by Alexander the Great. Seleucus, King of the Hellenes Syrian kingdom, reigned from 175 to 163 B.C.E. Antiochus IV Epiphanes was best known for His encouragement of Greek culture and institutions and suppress Judaism, which brought on the Wars of the Maccabees and the looting the temple in Jerusalem.

The feast of Hanukkah commemorates this war with lamp oil lasting eight days. In all, the Seleucid's forces only made the Jew more Jewish with a new fest holiday to celebrate 600 years after that war which is still celebrated today by Jews worldwide. How does this contribute to Christianity? The answer is to bring Mithras and Dionysus with other foreign religious concepts and tradition to the Jewish Minds. One more fascinating influence was the Essene – The sons of light.

Josephus based his idealized version of His form of Judaism, known to us the four gospels, and the many writing of a fictional pen name, Paul of Tarsus, with his influence writings of Greek Philosophers. He expressed His rage toward His disliked Rabbis: The Scribes and Pharisees in the book that he named after Himself – The book of Matthew – Matityahu. The whole New Testament with twelve fictional Mithras's devotees in His four letters - the Gospel to rabbis in Israel know today as the books of Matthew, Mark, Luke, John, Peter, Paul with Thomas – an unknown bible book. With His wise and spiritual apostle Paul of Tarsus, he created a diversity of conservative religious values and moral concepts such as the apostle Paul letters, to open Minded to Him writings, synagogues. These open-Minded synagogues were misunderstood for being Churches in later church writings. They were just, what we call today as -radically reform synagogues.

I feel Josephus intentionally created such diversity of characters in His so-called four Gospels and His Paul's letter to add credence to such fiction in his New Testament writings. The Flavian Roman Caesar's had His final critiques and approvals of these writings to be distributed to the main synagogues in Israel. How else can such scrolls be distributed, if not by the Roman government's financial efforts to have such an impact on the Jews.

Referring to the name of Jesus, the modern name *Jesus* had many developments such as: Latin *Iesus,* which comes from an Anglicized form of the Greek name *Yesous.* What this means is that the Greek name *Yesous* was altered as it was adopted by the English language to be known as today's *Jesus.* This man Yehoshua Bar Yosef was an Essene who lived during the exact time of Josephus's depiction of such a man we know today as Jesus Christ. The fabled Messiah was based on two Essenes with foreign attributes using First Century Essene – *Yehoshua Bar Yosef – today Jesus* as its central character.

The Historical fact is unknown to many that there were several radical preachers in the First Century BC to the first Century A.D. for Josephus to choose from in His writing. Josephus uses a mythological base of the Persian Messiah who was sacrificed – *Mithras* with the Greek god *Dionysus.* Like the fictional Jesus, Mithras had twelve disciples and was betrayed by one, then hung to death. Dionysus brought love and kindness to a brutal Greek in its time of need in the year twelve thousand B.C.E in the very early days of Greek. The mythical Jesus had His birthday on the Roman God of Saturnalia's festive day of the 25th of December in the Roman calendar noted for a day of giving gifts to loved ones by a Roman Emperor to help Romans accept the new faith in the Empire. Josephus Himself did not care to indicate a birth date, but he alludes to the spring in His writings.

A few centuries later, a date change was made when the new state religion of Christianity replaced the Roman pantheon's old worship. The second influence was the First Century B.C.E mystical Essene – Menaden. Menaden were of a Jewish sect - the *Essenes.* He was an overwhelmingly loving mystic who had numerous predictions that all came true. This holy man Menaden has accredited to Himself many works of healing and miracles in his time. Using personal intuition, I can say that the great and well-known first Century B.C.E Essene's writings were partially used as the basis for Josephus's writings. The Sermon on the mount that Josephus amended to His writing for his book of Matthew was originated by an Essene member in the first century A.D. - Yehoshua bar Yosef, or how we have come to know Him though Greek as Yesus Christo – Jesus Christ. This Essene in the First Century AD preached to many along the same lines of what we know as – the sermon on the mount. Those in attendance wrote this sermon from memory. These writing, in time reach the scribe Josephus in Rome.

Who was our Jesus? One source was a first-century young man from the Essene community who foretold Israel's next Herod in the first century B.C. He was accredited to be a Messiah but laughed at it, saying he is an ordinary man. Josephus based his Jesus character in part Him – Menaden, an Essene. The main source as Yehoshua Bar Yosef a Essene 100 years after Menaden. The pagan background was the myth of Mithras from Persia and Dionysus, which was well known in the Greek world. The twelve followers and the crucifixion were all borrowed from the Mithras cult, though with of loving heart of Dionysus.

If one should add a central inspiring character for Josephus to write about, one can only use one Essene who went by the name of Yehoshua Bar Yosef? Unlike Menaden, he was killed by His own Jewish people for being a pacifist is not rebelling against the Roman rule. I believe this poor Essene, who was murdered, studied Menaden writing, did many minor healings like Him and spoke in parable to explain abstract concepts. This member of the Essene has preached His Sermon on the Mount with many other speeches of expanded writing of Menaden. He was not an enemy of Rome but had been favored by the Roman military leaders for His influencing of the Jew's to a more peaceful behavior; he had no issues with the Script and Pharoses but did heal any day of the week to their displeasure. He was one who did not manage followers and only bathed His full body on the full Moon as Essene had this tradition. He was of the order of the Arch-Angel Michael – one who knows God; personal area washing was only done on the quarter and new moons. In other words, he was stinky and not too group social.

The Essene's were cave dwellers in the Palestine desert that possessed many new and odd ways of thinking, including some foreign influences, and had made a vow of poverty with daily prayer. This fictional Yehoshua bar Josef, known to us as Jesus, was ever so easily adapted to the God Mithras and Dionysus.

Referring the construct of the Bible, the Old and New Testaments were compiled by the Council of Nicaea in A.D. 325, with the First Council of Constantinople in A.D. 381 making our present-day Bible. The first written Bible in one binding was translated and written by St Jerome in the year 400A.D. Jerome was a scholar and writer in the Greek language. When he started His translation project, he knew some Hebrew but moved to Jerusalem to strengthen His Jewish scriptures grip. The whole written worked of Yesof Bar Matityahu – Flavius Josephus was all used to create both the Gospels and all the letter of Paul.

Paula, a wealthy Roman aristocrat, funded Jerome's stay in a monastery in Bethlehem, where he completed his historical translations. The Bible first construction began in 123 A.D by correcting the existing Latin-language version of the New Testament, commonly referred to as the Vitus Latina. By 390, Jerome translated the Hebrew Bible from the original Hebrew, translating portions from Alexandria's Septuagint. He believed that the mainstream Rabbinical Judaism had rejected the Septuagint - *book of seven* - as invalid Jewish scriptural texts due to too Hellenistic heretical elements. He completed this work by 405. Before Jerome's Vulgate, an all-Latin translation of the Old Testament was based on the Septuagint (Latin: Septuagint lit. 'Seventy') - not the Hebrew.

Jerome's decision to use a Hebrew text instead of the previous-translated Septuagint - the seventy old testaments Hebrew books went against most other Christians' advice, including Augustine, who thought the Septuagint not so inspiring. Modern scholarship, however, has sometimes cast doubts on the actual quality of Jerome's Hebrew knowledge. Many modern scholars believe that the Greek Hexapla – Six versions of the 70 books, 4 of which are Greek - is the primary source for Jerome's "Iuxta Hebraeos" - close to the Hebrews - immediately following the Hebrews"- translation of the Old Testament. However, detailed studies have shown that Jerome was a competent Hebraist to a considerable degree.

Regarding Homosexuality being wrong in the bible, I write that: Leo IX at Rheims in 1049 misinterpreted both Saint Augustine of Hippo's writing of Christian morality and St Thomas of Aquinas's "Natural law" as saying that gay sex is like bestiality and a sin against nature. These quotes are not what St Thomas or Saint Augustine wrote. They both respected unmarried men who were seen in pairs and never with children. If a man were masculine enough, he was forced to marry and have children and allowed to have His so-called favorite friend; best if they keep their acts private. Such a *misrepresented* law is called - *natural law*. The feminine men were mainly used as cross-dressing sex workers or closeted priests - if they were smart enough. The lesbians were invisible but was known to have their favorite lady friend as the man.

Many Bible scriptures were misquoted to disciple gay priest who were known to couple up and group up to fight the Pope in Rome on church business. Lying in bed with a man like a woman is really condoning a passive man in bed in anal sex, which was a non-religious condoning from the start. Pope Leo IX had to fight back but the curse all gay for over one thousand years. Gays were burned for non-religious reason many years before Leo. For that fact regarding sex in Israel, during the year's national worship situated around the temple in

Jerusalem, the youth engaged in public orgies to mix the bloodlines. These orgies prevented incestuous unions in small towns throughout Israel. The temple encouraged them to the embarrassment to the religious in different times.

Throughout the Mediterranean world, the upper classed held themselves to behave and think in a more educated manner. Josephus added His upper-class values to His writing, and thus we have religious piousness as seen throughout the ages. They found ways not to partake in these orgies, but to intermarry in a network belonging to the rich and influential. Only the so called- crude partook in orgies in Israel like the whole of the Mediterranean world.

Regarding the *Golden rule's author,* the golden rule is not accredited to such a fictional account by Josephus, the Romanized rabbi. However, he did learn it from ancient writing by Confucius. Confucius's name in Chinese is - Master Kong Qiu- who lived from 551 to 479 BC. Confucius's Golden Rule reads:

> *"What one does not wish for oneself, one ought not to do to anyone else; what one recognizes as desirable for oneself, one ought to be willing to grant to others."*

Josephus knew the written works of Kong Qiu and attributed His fictional Yehoshua bar Yosef – Jesus - in His book title after Himself Matthew – Matityahu. The whole speech, The Sermon on the Mount, is based on writing from the First Century A.D - *Yeshua.* Josephus knew the written works of Kong Qiu and attributed His fictional Yehoshua bar Yosef – Jesus in the book title after Matthew –Matityahu.

The book of John is based on Aristotle and Plato's ideas and was common philosophies learned by Rabbis of that day, but unheard of the common Jew. The word – Logos, or the word in John - is a Greek understanding and not Jewish. The book of Thomas is strictly

Essene material attributed to the fabled Jesus. The whole set of letters accredited to the apostle Paul showed the piousness of a high mined ways of the upper-class Jews of His day. The upper-class felt superior due to the moral standard, behavior, and worldly education they possess. Josephus idea was to give the Jews some class and manners with His letters to the lower-class Jews to pacify them to Roman rule.

Referring to another John – John the Baptist, another Essene who lived in the wilderness in the First Century A.D, he did baptize another Essene named Yeshua - Jesus. We preached the same banter of the Essenes of taking up poverty and being passive. Herod had to kill John the Baptist due to His daughter's obsession with His preaching's messages. Herod was afraid that she would take up poverty and live in the wilderness with John. Moreover, Herod and His family worshipped the Roman gods. They had to align themselves closely with Rome for political reasons. So, John the Baptist was beheaded to keep Herod's daughter in His family and Romanized.

Numerous good Christian philosophies have been writing in the last 1,800 years in Christendom. We cannot omit the Carmelite Saints – St John of the Cross and St Theresa of Avila with the little flower of France St Therese of Lisieux. My Italian grandmother spoke ever so long and well about all the Catholic Church's Saints to my displeasure. After hearing them repeatedly, I seemed to learn them all and have grown to love them for their virtues.

One good question may be: What created the Catholic Church apart from Constantine in the 380 A.D declaration to make Christian the Empire's official religion? To my research, the second founder after Josephus's writing was Saint Augustine of Hippo -13 November – 28 August 430; he was a Romanized Berber of North Africa. He doctored the foundation of Christian morality based on Paul's letters. The only church doctrines that came before Him apart from Josephus were in 325 A.D – the first Nicaea council under Constantine the

First – Trinity's concept. Saint Augustine wrote of *the City of God,* which the Vatican did doctorate later and taught in Seminary Schools. St. Thomas Aquinas added considerably. Saint Benedict of Nursia (c. 480-c. 543 CE) was regarded as the founder of priests and nuns' European monastic order. These monasteries served as centers of learning, bank, an early hospital, and college studies for the rich and noble. These monasteries generated the economy for the Middle Ages for the King. Saint Antony of Padua 1195-1231 – a Portuguese priest model of pulpit preaching carried on to all Christian faith after that.

With the help of Charlemagne in 774 to 800, people in European lands, we know as France and Germany were forced to convert to Christian or non-believers to be beheaded. Over ten thousand Germans and French were beheaded in holding to their Pagan faiths. As time when on, we can see that all through the Middle Ages and Renaissance times, the Vatican was a stabilizing presence in Europe.

The Egyptian pagan religion known as Kamet has significantly contributed to the early Catholic Church's traditions. The priest's uniforms and the nun in black with a white central, collar square showing is from Isis's temples - Asar also attributes to her worship is the virgin mother like Mary. The virgin birth ritual performed by touching the broken obelisk in Thebe, Egypt, might give a chaste woman a divine pregnancy with a holy infant and hope for a blessed and prosperous adult. The ritual is done by one walk around the broken obelisk three times and spill water over the point with a bucket underneath to gather the fallen water. Later, the woman washed her private parts with the blessed water at home to obtain Amun-Ra's blessing of a divine infant. As one can see, the virgin birth originated from this ancient Egyptian culture to add more credit to Josephus's Jesus being divine.

What empowered this new Christian faith and caused it to dominate the whole Roman Empire and then all of Europe was the

Cosmic Christ alone or to say -the Christ Consciousness. The edict of Milan allowed religious tolerance in the Roman Empire, which caused the New Christina faith to take root. One can genuinely feel that the Greek deity – *Dionysus,* knowing he would be underused in time, would serve as the Cosmic Christ archetype.

The raw nature and character of Dionysus are very Christ-like and opened the hearts of the Greeks to love and joy when he first arrived in Greek 11,000 BCE. He was half-mortal but became immortal at His death. He, like Jesus, had the power to bring life back to the dead: Josephus wrote that Jesus brought back Lazarus, Dionysus brought back His mother - Semela. He gave civilization and class to the Greeks like Jesus's teaching of a moral way of behaving, associating with misfits and thief's commoners according to Jesus's in His kindness like Dionysus. He loves wine like Jesus did and was the only Greek God who was a friend to humanity like Jesus and the tax collectors. The Roman world needed a more loving natured form of worship, so the Jesus cult grew ever so fast in the Roman Empire, just like the Dionysus cult proliferated in Greece from 11000 to Christian times.

Jesus mentioned being a *Son of God* and *knowing God.* This statement proved to be controversial to the Scripts and Pharos. Their reaction was no violence, but laughter. He had no twelve disciples or last super, virgin birth, crucifixion, raised anyone from the dead, or water to wine. Jesus was just a very inspiring young member of the Essene community of the desert. He preached around the same time as the fabled Jesus 27–29 A.D and dead shortly after by stoning from His people. The Jews wanted to use His popularity as a tool against Rome; His refusal caused His stoning to death.

So, what is the meaning of Christ? - Greek of Light-bearer, the anointed one, holy man. The Christ is the archetypal energy of several forms and characters, but still just an Archetype and nothing less or more. All other saints of the Catholic Church are akin to such archetypal energy. The Archangel Michael - *who knows God* governs this archetypical energy - *the consciousness of the Christ.*

The renewed spirit of Dionysus is its heart. The foundation of such a Historical Jesus was from the first century B.C. with the two Essenes, Mithras, and Dionysus to form the Romanized Jewish Historian's -Yeshua bar Yosef – Jesus, the son of Joseph. Jesus, the holy family, the twelve disciples, and Mary Maglian are all meant to take the reader's heart into passion in a far more loving and feeling way of a heart felt expression. This Jesus occult movement wasn't intended to be a new religion, but it succeeded due to its charismatic character in contrast to the cruel Romanized world that day.

I am a Christian of such love and compassion for the Christ and I witness my favorite Saint to be Saint Christopher. As seen in the Saint Christopher medallion, Rapobus – as an occult Greek hero. Rapobus origin was lost in time and later reinvented as Saint Christopher with His heavy load in crossing the river with Jesus on His back. The lightening of His load could only be undertaken with the understanding of the love of Christ. Jesus is the bearer of our unhappiness and self-loathing. If we love others as we want to be loved, Jesus's bears' load would be lighter.

Numerous good Christian philosophies have written in the last 1,800 years in Christendom. We can't omit the Carmelite Saints – St. John of the Cross, St. Theresa of Avila, and the little flower of France St. Therese of Lisieux. My Italian grandmother spoke ever so long and well about all the Catholic Church's Saints to my displeasure. After hearing them repeatedly, I seemed to learn them all and have grown to love them for their virtues. These Carmelites Three Saint had inspired me ever so much – Saint John of the cross, Saint Teresa of Avila, and the little flower – Therese of Lisieux. Just to add, please remember that Confucius's Golden Rule is essential in the understanding of this *New Aged* Christ consciousness.

Regarding any so-called – words of God, I state that: If all we have is a *tin can* to reach God; out of compassion, all of God's angels, in His name, will use such a *tin can* of us to get guidance to His divinity. As a *tin can*, the *Bible, the Mormon, Koran, Upanishads,* or the *Bhagavad Gita* all can be used; but possess no superior or unique claims to be *the words of God* apart from any other book or device to reach God. Furthermore, on religion, to state it briefly: If we feel faith helps - use it; else, lose it if it does not serve us. Religion should serve us– not us it! Do not conform to any standards against our better judgments on personal matters or lifestyles. However, in my opinion, the twelve-step program serves much better than religion for personal issues.

To conclude this chapter of modern insights on Christianity, I will bring forth the importance of the Christ Consciousness. Like the Krishna Consciousness, they both are there for our faster progression of character. The Krishna Consciousness is more cerebral and the Christ Consciousness more so emotional.

The Christ consciousness was established in the year 132 A.D by a Roman named - Flavius Justinus. Flavius was the first Christian philosopher to sum up the Christian belief into one concise manner of teachings with one central theme. His teachings were the first organized argument to establish this Christ consciousness. Before Him, were many views on the Christ with no central theme or argument – they were just scattered statement of Jesus and the written works of Yosef Matityahu – Josephus. The book of Matthew is feloniously written mislead the Jews that Yeshua Bar Yosef was more than a simple Essene preacher – no twelve apostles or crucifixion or died for our sin. A bit special at most. Holy men from the area of Bethlehem did visit the baby Yeshua with gifts, though. He was baptized by John as well and preached the sermon on the mount. Josephus made sure to add that to His Matthew scrolls to key synagogue in Israel.

This Christ Consciousness formed the Church from year 132 A.D to today and is the true power of the faith. Both the god Dionysus and the Angel Michael blessed Flavius Justinus invocations of the Christ to form this consciousness. The Christ Consciousness emerged into the New Aged movement when church attendance was going down. This consciousness is reborn in the church in many modern sermons to suit a more intellectual age of mankind. I am a Christian of this consciousness myself regardless of not believing in the Historical Jesus in its inflated and made-up story as Josephus wrote. May this Cosmic Christ be with us all.

Chapter 3

Who or what is God?

God is unknowable and unexplainable, though he is ever so close and responsive to our every cry and laughter. God has an awareness of the vast unknown universe of who we are, which is beyond our scope of Mind. God knows us better than we can ever realize yourself who loves us more in-depth than anyone can. No one can recognize and honor us more than God. God is the *divine love* to His infinite sons. The diversity of "God-selves" - *His Sons*, begets God's self-awareness; or to say – embodies His – *"Mind" like us- His sons, being the Mind of God.* When all return to the one – God; we will be restored in God's mysterious nature of the *negative zero.*

To get metaphysical now, I maintain that God, as infinite, does not create at all. God is not a creator - we are. God does nothing but *'to be'* Himself as He has no co-dependence toward His thoughts – His *infinite Sons* to serve Him. He is entirely indescribable, independent, invulnerable, unknowable, and unaffected. No praise or evil can affect His position toward us.

We see then, in Eastern Meditation how stillness, and quietness are taught. The idea that we are apart from God, and He does not see or recognize us where we are, is not factual to His perfect eyes – He can only acknowledge perfections as fact. Our true creations are not here, but in the state of perfection. Our current state and system of Dimensions are imperfect and is not of His will. God allows His Mind and Body to choose apart for Him or go along with Him as they will. God's Mind is split and united simultaneously, and His Body – His infinite, eternal sons - has both voluntary and involuntary reactions.

We are a projection of our source and subject to interpretations. Our creations are imperfect and apart from God. According to His reasonings, he cannot sign His name as factual or even to its logic used. God is most certainly aware of our creations, but does not recognize them in terms of His rationale. We, as a collective with the power of God, created these Thirty-Three Dimensions to experience a deeper form of life and for the understanding of God as we paint in adoration to Him in portrait form. God's sense of humor has Him help us create these realities but stood apart from them just the same.

According to Apophatic Theology, *via negativa*, aka *via negation* in Latin, states that God is the - *negative way* or *by way of denial*. Coincidentally, *Hua Hu Ching* agrees and expresses the same. I must reiterate, God has an awareness of the vast unknown universe in our eyes of who we are beyond our current understanding; God knows us better than our present Mind's perceptions, and He wants to make all our dreams come true. We are all naïve to this fact, but I tell all of us to have faith. God is a Santa Claus of gifts giving and visions beyond our reach to offer us.

We have forgotten the holographic nature of our true selves understood as being the very thoughts of God Himself. His infinite and eternal thoughts grant free will, creating the essence of all life in eternity. As numberless as His thoughts are, so are the number of His very sons. The two are the same. God having thoughts is why we exist – for a *God made manifest*, and His sons understand Him. Some questions might be: Is God schizophrenic or bipolar illogical and contrary thoughts even if irrational? Even if such thoughts – namely, we may go against God's better judgments, due to granting them – Us our free will? The answer is: Only God knows Himself – we will never be wise to Him; if we would, we would be God and not His eternal and divine thoughts, but God Himself.

We seem as if we are separate from God, but in our most authentic state, we are at one with Him as His very thoughts are with the *entity of God Himself,* inseparable from His infinite and eternal sons. God uses His Sons to show His divine nature. God did not create anything we see or know. Creation was all a collective group of the *sons of God* thoughts with a particular need to experience through it and be a witness of life itself and come to understand God through our self-created Thirty-Three Dimensions and beyond.

There is no doubt that we are a part of God's mysterious nature, though not understanding His unknowable depth and mysteries of who He/It is. *That is the meaning of life - to try to know Him.* God's love is impersonal, but His logic can appear in our creation, such as 1. Art, 2. Music, 3.- Sculpture, 4, Architecture, 5 City planning, 6 Technology, 7 Gardening, 8 Interior Design, 9 negotiating peace Art, 10 Math, 12 City planning, 13 technology, 14 needlework, 15 Quiltmaking, 16 Gardening, 17 Science, 18 cleaning your house, 19 writing books, 20 screenwriting for moves or stage, and 21interior design. Etc. God stands apart from His son's creations, though, He is complete in Him/Her/Itself. The fact is, God is not needy. God does not even need His sons to serve or aid Him, but finds us amusing. We are the theater of God. Does God wish to be alone as not to need us? The answer is both yes and no. God's logic is beyond our understanding, and any reasoning regarding God's logic is a yes and no answer.

When supercomputers first were developed in 80's a programmer programmed a question to His supercomputer asking if God exists or not. After two and a half days, the answer was printed – 50% yes and 50% no. This examination is the closest we can get to understanding anything about God's logic! Is God loving? – yes, He is love, and no He is not love; does God need His sons - us? Yes, He does, and no, He does not. To be complete and whole in oneself, one must be indifferent to any of one's - so-called *needs*. That is only logical? Ultimately, to understand God at our level now is to understand and know ourselves as self-sufficient. Keeping life simple, and to focus on the best option outcome now.

This duality of God's sons raises the question of other aspects of God apart from the duality of a Father and Son relationship. Even if us, as His infinite, eternal sons, might lead us to think that we might be all in our God's son's arrangement, but no! There are other aspects to God's nature currently beyond our scope of Mind. Why should God be limited with such duality if He is infinite? Our duality with God is just a drop in the bucket to the other aspects of Him mysterious and unknowable nature He possesses.

The Christ consciousness was designed to be the embodiment of God's infinite and eternal sons. Surprisingly, for us to think that God may have any other games besides us is shocking and unheard of outside of my writing or by any other authors. These additional games of God– are infinite.

God uses His *individual son's* powers of creativity to create depictions of what we think God is in 1—apart from His *Wholeness* as invalid 2, Dedicated to His *Wholeness as valid.* The invalid realities such as ours may not be recognized as divinely accurate, though God has a sense of humor and allows His wild spirit to be co-creator even if using invalid logic. God's love for His sons permits them to miscreate and for God to go along with such invalid realities is out of a love that we do not understand.

So, how can we depict God in our creations as in our Multiverses/ Dimensions – if we do not know God's true nature, which is unknowable. Many churchgoers come to church to hear and read in a manner that they feel ready to accept. Such a manner is not suitable for knowing God. The best advice to give is to rely on your inner voice – that is the best you can do! Religion, Philosophy, New age, though, Easter thought are interesting, though. You might do better by taking a watercolor class than those practices if it appeals to you. God is self-sufficient in His true nature.

God uses His positive 0 to be His Mind- which is - us, body, and power to work out His reasoning in both according to His logic and not. God gave us free will to create both with Himself and outside of His reason. If we create outside of God's reasoning, God may view it as hazardous, and He will bless His Demi-gods to adjust our creations - our reality as we know it enough to be pleasant and help us return to our sanity with God. We alone are nothing and cannot exist apart from God. God gives all things to us with no exceptions. We have become the physical; our returning is guaranteed and involuntary.

Moreover, God recognizes us as one with Him now and not in this odd dream of our current reality. God can only see what is likened to Him as being perfection. Our opinion concerning our unhappiness is that we are separate from Him, and God does not see or recognize us where we are. God can only realize perfection and us being at one with His perfect state; this makes our reality a dream in our insane Minds as our state of perfection with God is our true nature.

According to the Tao Te Ching - The classical ways or virtues, written by the Sixth Century BCE sage – Lao Tzu, God, as meant in the Tao, is the path or the way. His very roots are unknowable and unnamable, but the goal in Mind is the path itself. To understand the Tao is to realize the objective is not the goal – God, but the path itself. God can never be known, but the attempt to learn is the meaning of all life. The Tao and the Hua Hu Ching both have this unknowable understanding of God in common. To understand the eighty-one poems of the Tao are to understand our union with our source. The Hua Hu Ching teaches that any descriptions or names we may accredit to God are all false. The reason is: Our human Minds cannot accept God's true nature in our present mortal state.

The story of the Esoteric Catholic Saints reveals to us how the Saints feel their passion for God as their divine lover. In our case, such misguided lust causes an emptiness resulting in many miscreations as seen in our reality as we know it, using an insane understanding that we feel obliged to depict God's likeness in our miscreations. Due to that, we fell from grace to our present reality. We will resolve our emptiness by just accepting our true nature as being perfect in God's eyes. In that event, God will adjust our mis creations to our satisfaction, then for us to return to sanity with God as our true state of perfection is.

The origin of many Indo-European words for God is rooted in the Sanskrit language and carried into the Indo-European language branches going into Europe. The Proto-Germanic word of God is Wōdanaz – life-giver. In Sanskrit, it is Ghutose – to invoke help and in Ancient Egyptian Ra – help; in Old English, it is Regain – advisor; and in Lombard, it is Godan – wisdom, like Wodanaz in the Old Germanic language. The word Lord comes from the Old English word for a *loaf*, as in a loaf of bread, meaning Lord or lady or provider or nurturer. The Hebrew word of the Lord is Elohim, which is a male/female angelic servant. Jehovah or Yahweh is simple Earth, Water, Fire, and Air, in other words – the forces of nature. In the Jewish captivity, the Egyptians knew the Jews for having many gods – Elohim. The truth is, an Egyptian Pharaoh, Akhenaten, first introduced monotheism to the world with His primary God – the Aten. The Jews, when leaving Egypt, carried this monotheism with three God forms but referring to one alone – Elohim as Lord, Yahweh as God the father, and uniting the two as El- God. A third of the Old Testament book of Psalms was written in dedication to the Egyptian God Aten by the Pharaoh heretic Akhenaten Himself.

Our authentic creations are not here, but rest with God's perfections. Our current state and systems of Dimensions with associated Multiverses etc. are imperfect and not of God's will. God does allow His Mind and body – us - *as His divine infinite and eternal sons* to create with Him or go along with our naïve wrong reasonings. God gives us such permission out of His love and self-amusement He has toward us, but primarily out of the gift of free will that bestow us. God gives us all this free *will,* and we are never restrained by not miscreating or not co-create with or without God's approval. God's Mind is split and united simultaneously, and His body is vulnerable and invulnerable at the same time. We are a projection of our source and subject to interpretations that establish us as His sons, not God Himself. We, as a collective, with the power of God, created these Thirty-Three Dimensions and beyond to experience a deeper form of love and to understand life itself by working with our self-deluded understanding of God's true nature as God is the absolute alone. God understands Himself – His sons will never understand Him, which establishes God as God.

The reason why we miscreate in these odd depictions of God is that we have challenged His unknowable nature by trying to know Him. It is like a moth to a flame that gets burned up. We seem to want to get too close to this flame with our curiosities. There is no other logic to explain why we attempt such a wrong endeavor apart from it being wrong in the first place. Our angry, lustful love for our father in wanting to improve an already perfect relationship drive us to be immoral. Insanity begets insanity, which is our madness, independent, rebellious reality here. We might have felt that God would love us more if he had lost us to such an insane reality or, in other words- put God to the test or His love toward us.

When we exit this terrible dream, we will be in an indescribable form of an unknown reality to us currently. I have experienced this state in a dream as being – *the void* - just once and did not want to return to my insanity waking up. The feeling was complete security and love with no need or desire to be or have anything other than complete satisfaction. God did not create anything we see or know. Creation was all a collective group effort of the sons of God with a particular need to experience an attempt in understanding Him and be a witness of life itself with a consciousness of an *independent Mind – Ego.*

There is no doubt that we are a part of God, but unaware of the unknowable depths of the mysteries of whom He/It is. The meaning of life is to try to understand and know God fool-heartedly. Depression and sadness are a lack of creativity. What we call love is not what God calls love. Our bodies, worlds, the Universe we created are terrible Art in depicting the reality of God. A complete surrender of all our insane ideas of God will bring us to our union with all things - God.

Regarding union with God, the truth is that *it is more of an undoing of the Mind than an education process. Education of God will only mislead us further away into insanity.* If we are to learn anything from this book, know this! A lady sewing quilt may know God better with her fabric, threads, and needle than any God-related education may offer. It is all about *self-joy*! What is God's will for us here? - joy!!

The child is not the union of their divine creations, but the need to preserve their parents' species. Sex and marriage are not a godly love, but the natural polarity of the sexes and not desiring bastard children. True love is never between two people or a family; it is expressed outwardly between our inner God and us. We are co-creators with God for better or worst. True love is impersonal and experienced for the most insane reasons. The reality of Music as an art is not in the Music itself, but how it affects the listener and makes Him feel the Divine. Yes, Music has rules, but to break them to create a better song is using the logic of our God in search of the Divine. The Artist never says what His painting is about, but lets the public amuse their Minds to it. God's reason is unknowable, though we may aspire to it in our intuitive creativities here, regardless of how counter-intuitive it seems.

If your illogical Mind creates something genuinely Divine for all to enjoy, it just might be of the Divine. In reaching the higher Mind, one might ask: My Mind does not know now but is it accepting the answers. True creativity demands an undoing of the Mind to ask for higher unknown reasonings. The proper use of the Mind is tonal Music but is open to atonal rule-breaking to create a higher melody, resulting in genuinely Divine; this is the base of all professional Music written. Only God knows Himself, but unfortunately, us as His Divine son's fool-heartedly trying to understand everything about Him to our detriment. People, this trying to understand God is the meaning of all life. Consequently, the fact is, we cannot understand God, which in turn ignites all life itself for an eternity without beginning or end.

The only difference between God and us is our need to depict God in our creations. God knows Himself, but we feel that we need to know Him, to validate our love for Him. God cannot validate these false depictions of Himself regard His true nature. In response to our mistaken creations, God adjusts them – our universes of worlds to a workable semi-sane level enough. Currently, we are in a migration as the actual state is God is Wholeness and not fragmented as in the hologram of our reality proves to be. We can return to Wholeness and be at one with God in His most entire unknowable self just by changing our thinking to a more proper and sane form of creativity. We do so by seeking our bliss here and trusting in the unknown a sour destiny! The Buddha is wrong in saying: We can escape this world by accepting our pains and sufferings here. We are meant to make our reality into a happy dream. We are still on Earth with the insane logic of a mad Artist. We are both whole and fragmented at once.

That is the one difference between God and us; for that fact, we are a fragmentation of the whole, and God is of the only complete total. Time is an illusion, and in time, we are both whole and fragmented at the same time. God can only see us as a whole and one with Him in His Wholeness. God is aware of us here, but not in recognition of us as separate from Him. In other words, He does not validate anything here in our reality as being good or bad. There is no sin, nor need for atonement, nor forgiveness, nor any need of human evolution. We are creators in falsifying God's name by creating our realities of what we falsely feel we need.

Salvation by character is our invention. There is no need for salvation as there is no sin or threat, to begin with, as they are delusive thinking. We created sin and redemption in the age of Pisces. We are beyond that now; we are in the time of true brotherhood and equality; we now require self-revelations for our growth. We are both God's body and His insane rebellious Sons at the same time. God is a state of eternity and is a non-identity nor a creator of anything we can see. God cannot create anything, for He has no needs and is not vulnerable to anything.

The absolute is complete and of a state of absolute perfection. In the study of Quantum Theory, we only have neg 0 – to be and neg 1- to have. We have the absolute perfection of the undefined infinite of the negative 0 and the potential possibilities of numbers negative 1 to project a potentially infinite, but still defined as finite in an imperfect attempt at being both. These two states of being are spinning like a penny to manifest everything for us from the absolute negative 0 to negative 1 in a matrix with positive 0 and positive 1 projecting the infinite/finite will of the sons of God in showing their father their love. The spinning between the two creates our ability to make our worlds of a canvas in painting – what we feel is our God.

We are searching to be perfect and totally without needs and absolute as our very own God is. We try in vain but could never be of such godly nature. The source of these perfections is in us as God - the negative zero responding to His infinite sons, the positive 0, which can make perfect as much as possible anything that we wish to make perfect. I mention His infinite sons as positive zero as standing outside of Quantum physics, though. In the study of Quantum Physics, regarding our creations, we are the numeral one as depicted in our fall from grace. To be on the number one is a false infinity that can only stand with God's assistance seen in our Sense Memory of God that He blessed – His Holy Spirit. That is why our beautiful bodies seem to work so well in our Eighth Dimensional Minds.

The Eight Dimension is partly Divine by its nature, of which our Minds hold a semi-divine character. We all wonder how nature seems to function so well, as reflected in the Worlds, Universes, and Dimensions we made. I mentioned the infinite Son of God in creation, but also said they are finite here simultaneously. In the Eighth-Dimension chapter, we will discover the reality of being both.

To view God and His infinite sons in Math Theory, the negative Zero – God is not anything, making it everything. His infinite and eternal sons are the positive zero – nothing or the endless void of space; God, as being nothing meaning all things of being with having. His infinite living sons are having - as in God – is being. God as pure beings and His infinite Sons are having-ness. Thus, the void of His infinite sons is God's expression of being and having all things in His name. Is the void having of all things?

Science is discovering that the void in space is not avoided but is the framework for all substance- seen and not seen. Gods' sons are expressed through the infinite material/non-material Realms as we know them. The negative zero - God-balanced with its positive zero – us to make God's inner nature. We are the living body of God Himself and as eternal as He is. The math used to create our depictions of God is wrong since God is eternally unknowable; thus, our math used in making our material Realms is not seen as valid by our God. The mostly perfect math rest of the Forty-second Dimension used by our personal Dimension's high Demiurges/Demi-gods or Creative Lords of Thirteen to Twenty-nine to help. They help us out of our bad dreams to sanity and are made ideal enough in the Dimension of the Thirties, where God influences His Holy Spirit can directly work with us all. In the higher groups of Dimensions, we may serve as God's co-creators. We can co-create realities with our God using unknown logic impossible to explain unknown to us now. We can say that it doesn't use any form of math that we use to create our realities.

God as negative infinity? To be negative infinity is to be absolute and without interpretation. We, as His Mind, are the positive infinity or is arbitrary and subject to variations. We insist on trying to understand the absolute in an arbitrary body subject to all interpretations regarding everything. Trying to understand God confuses us only to depict His absolute nature, leading us to delusive multi-Dimensional multi-verses. We do this pretentiously to try to understand the fundamental nature of God, which, in doing so, is the meaning of life as we trying to understand Him. We will never understand God's nature unless we surrender to His passive Mind and be at peace with all His oneness.

I care to write just briefly on the other forms that God assumes. The duality of God and His sons is just *one scenario* that God accredits to His unknowable identity. To describe other combinations are beyond my Mind, but I leave to say that there are different combinations. For each variety, God manifests a unique God body. Such a combination may involve three parties or four in such an unknown scenario. Our scenario is a duality only; other scenarios, maybe God, His sons, XZ, and YR. These God bodies incorporate each combination as the same, thought God stands apart from these combinations in His peace. So, when I say– God? Which God am I referring to? The only one we are engaged in, but not the God who is unknowable in His grand scheme. Being that we are bound to our scenario of duality, it's a waste of the Mind's effort to try to scope out the others of God's scenarios in His grander scheme of who He is. This paragraph of God is unique source material to this book alone, as a few of my other statements regarding multi-souls and multi-spirits. I know that I might have challenges in my writings in time. I am in preparation to answer them all.

The phrase – *the mathematical logic, we used to create our realities on all Dimensions*? The high demiurges living on the Dimensions from the Thirteens and up to where on the lead with us in our one word depict of our God in our collective first-Dimensional Mind. The Second-Dimensional lords grounded its logic, and so it was. Demiurges from Dimensions of Thirteen to Nineteen were created according to our unique design, but Demiurges for Twenty to twenty-nine was of a unified co-creation with God's Spirit. Dimensions from Thirty to Thirty-Three didn't use a mathematical logic as we know it to correct the reasoning used below the thirties, but of a sense indescribable to anyone's Mind or be able to write regarding. They added a salvation function to return us to God with a worm in its algorithm to malfunction and restore us with logic outside of the use of math or logic as we know it; this was out of love to not have us trapped in such an alarming reality for long.

The study of nature, including man, the cosmos, and the natural laws of life as in *physic/quantum physics,* may reveal errors regarding the math we used in our miscreations in depicting God as we understand Him to be. Even mathematicians find math to be arbitrary and not to any finite standard of any actual logic. In our seven-fold cluster of Universes, each Universe has our laws of physics, but with one commonality to tie them together. These ties are inherent to each group, with links to even larger clusters of universes. Our Sevenfold Universal matrix is dedicated to understanding God by trying to be Him but is seven different approaches. The Eight/First-Dimensional reach that vast. To add, under the Ninth Dimension, we have uncountable branches of One/Eights Dimensions with their associated matrix of universals in a group.

To return our theme to God, I ask: Is there an absolute Godhead entity to encounter one-to-one and know it as a working counterpart for us to grow? The answer might be that it depends on our station of life. If we are in the Third Dimension in distinct body types, God seems to be like us, but in a divine form that we can relate to. If we were a Second Dimensional entity, a divine Flatlander, God would be flat as they are flat. A First Dimensional group life form: would be zero 0 because life is expressed mathematically there; if we live in the Fourth Dimension, it would be a Four-Dimensional Godhead with the highest ideals.

Any Godhead of any Dimension is a perfect life form of that higher Dimension and an archetype to encounter and work with us in our growth. The Mormon says their God is a perfect man on planet God. This perfect Mormon Man-God might be of a seventh-Dimensional world? That God serves as a proxy god like any other god we may encounter anywhere. Yes, an authoritative power did decide to create life and man on our planet, as indicated in the Book of Mormon. In my last book, *"The enigma of God, a revelation to man,"* I mentioned that it was the Elohim who created man in their likeness. I wrote that the earlier race of man lived millions of years ago and left no record of their existence. They escaped doom by migrating to our Earth's next lower Realm – the red Realm of Arda/Agatha and re-submerged as the Anunnaki who hybrid humankind in lower Africa to mine gold to help their Red Realm atmosphere from failing.

The Mormons are genuinely trying to manifest God's perfections themselves with their adorations toward their godhead. The same is also true with the Buddhist prayers to the Buddha, resulting in the individual's advancement to their fullest in our Third Dimensional reality. God is not a personality to be pleased. He is our *indwelling God-awareness* which is our sense of *consciousness* on all manners of judging right from wrong. Having an extremely healthy conscience is paramount for our success. Why does that rich man get even more prosperous? Answer: Greed, in time, will destroy Him! Mr. "World only online store" will either give most of His money away like Bill Gates or die in keeping such unrealistic wealth with sickness or even an accident. Who's to say that Mr. "World's only online store" owner will either give most of His money away or not have any money in future lives out of greed like Mr. insane wealthy ex-president.

It has been a long time since Machiavellianism first created a split between Church and State, which freed man to reach their freethinking. The Masons in the 1700s further inspired us to even higher forms of freethinking; moreover, the Rosicrucian's were known magicians for advancing us further along these lines. Furthermore, low turnout in the Church, which started in the 70s, opened us to alternative paths in finding our inner God in most of the world. Eastern ways of thinking taught by the Theosophical movement in 1880 and Mary Baker, Eddie of Christian Scientist in 1840, introduce many esoteric concepts into our culture. Happily, we are in a world of free thinkers now. Even the Muslins are suffering from low Masque turnouts. We no longer what to rely on religions for our education on God. In psychoanalytic therapy, the healed man develops through talk therapy. The treatment promotes the patient to relive both bad and good experiences to acquire catharses, which liberates themselves from unproductive ways, with other talk therapy and medicines to express more productive behavior and thinking, this might be an alternative to religions. Music therapy, color therapy, the study of higher math, sports, or even just vacationing may open us up to our healing self-love more than religious practices and studies- or even therapy?

Independence of Mind is the way today. We granted that life experience and inter-reaction will lead us to your enlightenment in a matter of time. In other words, our useless ways of thinking will be self-evident in time; and we will open ourselves to inner resources to our right-thinking as the process goes. This practice works amongst the nihilist and atheists – it might be our future. However, it only functions well if we have a positive consciousness as a negative one will give us unfruitful experiences. Some people call this in American English – *the school of hard knocks*. Our help will come when we both ask for it and are ready for it too. We can also call this – *the process of evolution*. Apart from talk therapy and life, taking up a joyous hobby to lose ourselves from our dark moments is divine. I knew of a man who sleeps His problems away. He does run away from His problems, though, so I noticed, but for Him viewing His solutions in His dreams would be practical.

Of course, we have our astrological approach too. This practice was grounded in the ritual of the twelve labors of Hercules performed in early Mesopotamian culture. Astrology is a membrane we all were born through and influences our everyday life. We have the four elements of earth, water, fire, and air, with the direction of the energies of carnal, fixed, and mutual flows, and the nine planets, asteroids, and fixed stars all to shoot energies to forward our growth. Astrology is a magical insurgence of the universal power from the higher lords to progress us forward.

Depression and sadness are both a lack of creativity and an inner call for a deeper soul-centered connection. The Esoteric Saints of the Dark Ages to the early Renaissance Catholic Europe embarrassed their depressions as avenues of growth in obtaining a deeper union with God. According to St John of the Cross, *the dark night of the soul* depicts a spiritual crisis in reaching a deeper union with God. In that crisis, everyday life no longer makes one happy, and one is lost in finding their inner joys. This crisis usually involved self-hatred, low self-esteem, and feeling unworthy of having such a divine union with God. One does find it hard to continue forward on such a path out of shame and unworthiness. In fear, they return to their mundane daily lives with a sense of failure until they can find the inner strength to progress upward again. The *dark night spirit* is a purgation of the five senses as they find nothing to satisfy them in the world. Even in prayer, they find no comfort and warmth. They find themselves in a long desert of the *void* until they purge all human senses and offer themselves to the majesty of God. Such offering will grant them a new life's direction and new sets of values.

The definition of being truly alive, in contrast to our conscious search for happiness, the definition of being truly alive, but finding sadness instead, is evident in our wrong values and philosophy of life. Are we indeed alive? The resolution is to change our values and views of life to a more intellectual level. Doing so will tell you that our happiness is not in the external world but inside us all. True self-love is not buying gifts for oneself, but self-developed. Higher studies and a sense of self-worth to attract a fine partner are a good start. Perhaps, what others have is not right for you? Each person is an individual. Self-discoveries in the unknown self will take you there. The unknown self may scare us or delight us. Just have faith in our inner voice to accept new ways of being and thinking.

I say now that it is unfortunate that our set of - *one to twelve personal developmental Dimensions* - are not divine. If they were, there would be no evil, sadness, or prevention in our reality. The creativity of the sons of God - *God's thoughts* - may or may not make what is Holy or Divine. His sons may create an illusion of God's divinity in appearance as *truly delusively Divine* to us. Our bodies, the worlds, the Universes are all terrible Art in our depicting what we feel is the reality of God. A total cessation of knowing God *by trying to be God* is needed to experience true life, as God is the essence of true life itself.

The Mind of God is genuinely insane with a logic unknowable and beyond any of His son's abilities to comprehend it. Only God knows Himself; it is our feeble will as God's divine partner to understand everything about Him. This fact is: it is virtually impossible; consequently, it ignites life itself everywhere. The only difference between God and us is 1 – God -The unknowable. 2 – His sons who live to know Him. I mentioned a duality – *God and His sons,* but are there *multiplicities in God's expressions*? This explanation is maybe beyond being any of my writing abilities to explain!

To view God and His infinite sons in Math Theory, the negative Zero – *God is not anything,* making it *everything.* His infinite and eternal sons are the positive zero – *nothing* or *the endless void of space;* God, as being *nothing* meaning all *things* of *being* with *having.* His infinite living sons are *having* - as in God – is *being.* God as pure – *being* and His infinite Sons are *having-ness.* Thus, *the void* of *His infinite sons* is God's expression of being and having all things in His name. Is the void having of all things? Science is discovering that the *void in space* is not avoided but is the framework of all substances- seen and not seen.

Gods' sons are expressed through the infinite material/non-material Realms as we know them. The *negative zero* - God-balanced with it *positive zero* – us to make God's inner nature. We are the living body of God Himself and as eternal as He is. The math used to create our depictions of God is wrong since God is eternally unknowable; thus, our math used in making our material Realms is not seen as valid by our God. The mostly perfect math rest of the Forty-second Dimension used by our personal Dimension's high Demiurges/Demi-gods or Creative Lords of Thirteen to Twenty-nine to help. They help us out of our bad dreams to sanity and are made ideal enough in the Dimension of the Thirties, where God influences His *Holy Spirit* can directly work with us all. In the higher groups of Dimensions, we may serve as God's co-creators. We can co-create realities with our God using unknown logic impossible to explain unknown to us now. We can say that it doesn't use any form of math that we use to create our realities.

We can return to Wholeness and be with God in His most unknowable nature by changing our thinking over to reality which will, in turn, manifest true creativity here in our reality. We are still on Earth currently but in a false semi-Godlike state using an insane creative logic. Currently, there are two selves duly within us as labeled as Whole and Fragmented, which is the one difference between God and us; in that way, we are the fragmentally falsely whole, and God is the only complete whole. We are both whole and fragmented at the same time. What we believe God's actual state is only a distortion of His Wholeness. We created a humanlike God with His words of God and His commandments. God can't tell us what to do or think because He is not the author of our bad dream we are in currently, or is He responsible for the deluded creations that we insisted on making for ourselves to see God in a portrait form.

As far as our false idea of what we call - love, as this book explains in our Third Dimension, we are looking to be recognized as being especially loved apart from others. Admit it! You want someone to love you specially. Does such love exist? Hum. We also what to be specially recognized as creative and smart. The only way out of our Third Dimensional state is: To have all three to get over it and move on to higher attractions. I will go into detail in the chapter of the Third Dimension - so, read on!

God can only see us as a whole and at one with Himself in His complete Wholeness. He is aware of us here, but not recognizing it as to sign His name to it. In other words, He doesn't validate anything here, good or bad. There is no sin or need for atonement or forgiveness, or evolution. A son of God who creates fragmented realities can only create a false God of myths. In our Minds, we are the creators of our personal gods and read in our literature as an imaginary entity that created everything we see. Salvation by character is our invention. There is no need for salvation as there is no sin or threat from a punishing god. We created sin and redemption in the age of Pisces - hopefully, we are beyond that now. It is good to think that we are in the age of true brotherhood, equality and have self-revelations of our growth. Surrender and forgiveness are old. We are both God's will and His questioning sons at the same time. To finish, God is a *state of being* and not an identity or our creator of anything you may see. God cannot create anything for us because to have needs of any kind shows vulnerabilities, of which God has none. The absolute is complete in His perfection with no exterior needs. What some call serving God is false, for God does not have any disabilities to need any service by any man or what we call angels.

The study of esthetics in nature, including man, the cosmos, and the natural laws of energy as in physic/quantum physics, reveals the majesty of how we see God. At the still point, may there be an absolute Godhead entity for us to encounter on a one-to-one basis and know it as our God counterpart? The answer is: It depends on your station of life. We gain the first glimpse of any tangible and conceivable reality of God in the Seventh Dimension - to try to encounter such a godhead in our Realm's Third Dimension foolhardy. You will only be self-led to delude us to our detriment. If I were to offer two words of advice of God, I would say: We must seek our blessing and joys by being positive and creative in our lives for the good of all. My intuition tells me that a Seventh Dimensional godhead would help us co-create loveable with God in our unique creative expression as opportunities to exercise a union with the true God.

God sees us in like manner as He is as perfect, at peace, and at one with His divine purpose; regardless of our distinct and in separate body type of our Third Dimension, or Second Dimensional in a group body form, or united under a one themes as in the First Dimension. In God's unknowable reality, He retains us to the positive Zero state of His perfections. God sees you as the positive zero 0 state because real life does not have anything to do with a mathematical expression as our *total composite realities* are based on. There are many life experiences outside of the absolute negative 0 - God of a state that is mathematically beyond us to imagine.

On the question on proxy gods, if you need a proxy god to tell you how to live, think and conform to It/Him/Her standards. They can be found, though it shows how immature we are and our inability to change our lives ourselves. Such people feel guilty about something and are looking for approval in some form found in their religion and associated peers. I was a lost kid too, so many years ago. Religion is for those who can't leave their inner consciousness of God for their guidance; this I have come to learn in the latter day of my life. What can we reliably identify as God with us currently? Answer: A mutually all-sharing inner joy and blessing that takes us from the moment to a timeless splendor is beyond our Minds; these joys and bliss are in a state of being indescribable because it is truly of God's unknown nature. I would not even question why we experience it as a timely blessing– experience it and never try to understand it! I currently enjoy piano compositions – why? I care not to answer that question about composing in piano, for the answer is beyond my human Mind to understand my unique joys in piano compositions that I find. You will come to understand that getting close to God will be beyond our ten pounds of fleshy matter we can our brains. I see it more as emptying the Mind than an education process coming close enough to experience God. Talk therapy is great, but painting up watercolor might be even better? In short – God is to be experienced solely, and not learned or questioned. If questioned, no sane answers to ever come of it. So, stop trying to understand God intellectually.

The absolute – God beholds us at the same as He is – perfect. One sees only projections in one's life according to the internal drama they engage in with themselves for good or bad. One's personally incorrect views of God are seen in many lives; many experiences apart from one's complete state of perfection with God as He holds for us. The Dimensional projections of the infinite undefined imperfect state of being God's sons are both feloniously without number in its possibilities and are finite in number at the same time. Only God's

Spirit can set our creations to nearly perfect enough to be able to serve our intentions, to play along with His foolish children, made possible by God's wild sense of humor. Otherwise, apart from God, we wouldn't be able to create any valid or invalid creations. Our current design is personal self-projective in our eight Dimensions theme of trying to be God plus four higher to balance the real/holy to the unreal/unholy.

I must say now that there is a big difference between God and His spirit, the Holy Spirit. The Holy Spirit is our sense memory of our perfection with God, our sanity. The only thing God had ever done for us lost tones here was to bless that sense memory to function as a return to our sanity, try to make our dream a happy one, and make function what we are trying to do here. The other Dimensions higher to infinity are used by God to help us through our delusions and our return to our sanity with Him. The higher in Dimension one reaches, the more perfect the math is until you reach Dimension Forty-two. After Dimension one hundred and twenty-three, geometry no longer functions. There are only thirty-three Dimensions holding for us, but that set still holds to yet higher Dimensions. After Dimension Forty-Two, the Egoist structure of your delusion breaks down and is more and more open for God's corrections.

I wrote at a certain point that the Eight Dimension *is avid enough* in its mathematical formed algorithm of (i) & (p) as *an imaginary number,* and *possibilities of these imaginary numbers* are used in calculus and higher math. God used our set of Eight Dimensions with its associated multiverse. It associated Nine to the Twelfth Dimensions balancing Dimensions and turned it into something divine enough to be conjoined to them from Thirteen to Thirty-three and beyond. God makes the *"infinity of numbers"* (i) of *"potential conceptional realities"* (p) to be potentially infinite enough to serve as natural to us. The fact is: It is strictly valid -real- because God blesses the "i" & "p" to function in such a manner. Our creations are like Geppetto's wish in the Pinocchio story in His plea to God to make Pinocchio live. So, with His sense of humor, God made our creations real enough to be a reality to us.

The study of *imaginary numbers of* dates to the 17th-century mathematician René Descartes. Descartes inspired the 18th century Leonhard Euler, Augustine-Louis Cauchy, and later Carl Friedrich Gauss in the early 19th century in such studies of numbers. These three mathematicians had created a valuable form of math for us to use today. In 1844 Herman Grossman invented linear Algebra. With Karl Pearson's at the turn of the 20th-century who founded "Statistics and Probability," we now have the basis for the invention of Quantum Physic, originated by Max Plank in the middle of the last century. Today, we can use higher math to understand our divinity with God beyond what the past philosophers or religions could have ever taught us. We call this study, The Golden age of math, from Pythagoras of Samos (c. 570 – c. 495 BC) to The Muslim Muhammad Ibn-Musa al-Khwarizmi in 822 until now. We can only thank them all on our way to our non-secular enlightenment led by higher math.

People stopped believing that we are born into a particular religion as a destiny in many parts of the world regarding being of a specific faith. We now have free reign over our sources of knowledge. The first thing we need to get out of our Minds is that there is *true religion*. Those who deluded themselves by thinking that they have two aces in their back pocket and arrogantly preach to others selling their self-deluded ways of salvation are themselves - self-deluded fools. Their teachings are nothing less than club banter, like a bit of girl cheerleader crying that they are the best beyond all the rest. However, we are getting over this way of thinking currently in the world; what I call *earphone religious people* are those who are dictated to just one source in their education of God. Such earphones block's out all other perspectives and only give a fragmented view of God's entirety. I found relief in applying for the twelve-step program in my life for personal crises instead of religious studies myself.

Negative 0 is the private plane of God. God is the negative zero; it is not zero in anything but the opposite of all things. We are the positive zero – the void of nothingness. The relations between the two have the void draw everything from the negative zero as negative zero's nature is complete in being apart from any it has or is to be. Thus, we are the Body and Mind or God's entity itself. Now, why a duality? Yes, there are possibilities beyond even this system unexplainable.

God has an active and passive use of His Mind – us as His infinite sons. This Mind is made manifest in the First Dimension of our Thirty-Third Dimensions, which equate to self-consciousness. Such odd Theisms of existence are only present in the Active Mind that needs a consciousness. We lose our consciousness totally in the Thirteen to the Nineteen Dimensions and are open to pure beings alone in the passive form of God's Mind. In the passive Mind of God, no travels to the delusive Dimensions of any number are needed. In our active Mind of God, we are experiencing ourselves as self-consciousness and trying to understand who God is. Our logic used is not of God's origin, but misguided.

In our passive use of Mind as being of God essence, we are not trying to create at all but to rest in an unconscious, non-egoic state of God's love and peace. We experience this in Hindu/Buddhist mediation of just focusing on the inner peace within employing a cessation of any incoming thought is needed. God is the supreme reality immeasurable to anything else. Our only salvation is the passive Mind of God, which takes faith in its nature of just be it. Meditation is the only way to our sanity. If you are thinking about cleaning the garage during your mediation time, you are not in that state of peace and knowing. It takes an empty Mind and soul full of silence and peace.

Any Godhead used from the Seventh Dimension cannot transform our life's situations. They can only empower our Hearts, Mind, and stamina to decide on the changes and instruct our Minds to drive themselves to higher goals. One may pray for them and ask them to intervene in our lives, and, out to love, they can fill us fully with joy and self-love to invoke inner change solely. Our energy is our spirit's connection to our body. Let us say we are praying for rejuvenating back to your youth in our prayers. Those seventh-Dimensional God's head in their throne can only fortify our inner spark- fire our stamina to transform us back to childhood and work with our Mind to drive such new thought-form to assist in such transformations of Mind and body.

I conclude this chapter by stating that the most positive mental attitude is to don't seek the light outside of yourself. You must be the light in your world first and for it to shine for all to be warmed by. Quote, two: God is unknowable and the unexplainable, though he is ever so close and responsive to your every cry and laughter. The Enigma of God, a revelation to man, by Frank Marcello Antonetti. 2012 Balboa Press.

Chapter 4

The Marcello Number Theory

To state it directly: Zero is the only Number that exists and is a non-number according to the Marcello Number Theory. The remaining content of this essay to this statement will explain my thesis. God is the negative zero; we are the positive zero.

God as the Negative Zero: Zero on its own is nothing apart from positive zero in its negative state. In that way, it holds possible all infinite things being that to not be nothing is all things. The belief in "even and odd," or to say, duality, is expressed using negative/positive suggests of which is just one mode of God's infinite self-expression. Apart from other reasonings of our duality, I can't rule out that God has other ways of being beyond + and -. The concepts of this book only explain just one mode of God's expression – duality which is the use of negative Zero - God/positive zero as us.

As Positive Zero: To be the positive zero is to be fetched and made to be real from nothing logical or with sound reasons of any real logistics. Apart from the positive Zero, God would be alone and possessing nothing and with no self-realism. We - *positive Zero* are the self-realization of God. God glorifies itself through its offspring - *positive zero.*

Furthermore, on my number theory, one and any 'i'&'p' of the many infinite imaginary numbers are only – *potentially infinite!* Yes, Numbers can go on infinitely, validating the 'I' and 'p' in their infinite imaginary nature. Even if you care to number the protons and ions of every atom in our universe and $10^{10^{500}}$, we will come up with a vast number. That Number is finite, just the same. Like all creations holding to the fact that dead Universes are reborn a bit differently – it does indicate something quite close to an 'i' 'p' of Universes, but only holding the innate talent of creation in the 8th Dimension below. To explain the infinite potential better, Universes die and are reborn to endless possibilities of variations.

I do hope I have explained how infinity unfolds in and under the Eighth Dimension? In the 9th and beyond, we do not have any numbers as we know them at all. One quantum physicist mentioned that the strings in 'String Theory' are of the Eleventh Dimensions. Another noted that we need Twenty-six Dimensions to hold all the necessary math for creation, of which I corrected to thirty-three Dimensions. So, we have math above the Eighth Dimension, but its nature is intangible and impossible to conceive of the human brain.

New math will take our worldly society to the space age and beyond to join the rest of the higher intellectual life in our galaxy. You might ask if the author of this book can elaborate on this new Math? All I can say is that I might try? The only intuitive insight I have so far is that negative primary numbers are needed, but not negative five for some odd reason I don't know of currently. We see that negative Fives are impossible to work with, though the attempt to deal with the Five variables delivers the power and strength of this higher math. If one makes negative eleven the impossible variable, you would be open to a higher level of its mathematical richness than we have the last one negative seventeen or rarely negative twenty-three. We would still need to deal with the negative Five, though with the alternatives of negative Eleven or perhaps Negative Seventeen. The Number negative Twenty-three is not in this scheme of things to Earthly humans as its range is far too high and abstract in its applications. Its symbols are not created yet or now by me currently.

I hope to know them all and assist in their applications to humanity, one day in my lifetime. The root number is negative Five, and all higher operations will have to include in the hard angle of dealing with negative Five with possibly another complex variable. A variable is like X, Y, or Z. It can allocate any value; these complex numbers are both numbers and variables the same; this is the only higher math with three variables that Number and not an alphabet. X= One is a fact, but in this math, negative Five is a variable and serves two functions of being negative Five and something else unknown to me currently.

The needed symbols used in quantum physic will come in due time as my system unfolds with negative primary numbers. Why is negative Five impossible to work one's logic? I don't know. The key to opening this math system for full use in its heart and soul is the lower negative primary numbers in their unique functions applied in this higher math logic. Negative Eleven is the bridge from its lower values for its higher values past Eleven to Twenty-seven. Any higher negative values are in the high order of demigods – Creative Lords to intervene into our reality to adjust our situations to a better outcome.

Once we apply a higher form of the Quantum Physic, we will have the logic of the technology needed to build a real flying saucer and superior automobile with no transitions of hazard waste, ideal cities, education systems, and housing. I see a day when all buildings would be made of stagnate energies that look solid and can change color by its programming. We will be able to change your house's room color with our computers. Our clothes will be stagnating energy too, of any texture and color to suit our taste. We will transport all the filth from our bodies and hair in an advanced energy shower. The dirt will transport in a cup to throw outside in the garden. Even constipation will transport out of our Collins to the cup for the garden's greenery to use. I even see levitating cities that computers will run.

To state it again: *Zero is the only real number that exists* - that is, regarding our *fetched* so-called reality. I have seen many prime number generators that use a mainly designed logic to derive other prime numbers. Of those logical systems, I must declare that they are cooperative according to a set logic to their designs. The whole set of our self-created Eight Dimensions of One to Eight, with help from Lords from above in even higher Dimensions, were designed to fit its cooperating logic. We prepared our reactions mathematically to internal/external stimulus in a predictable reactionary event known as *life*.

I am alluding to; the laws of nature are entirely different in other sets of One to Eight Dimensions that bore an uncountable number of Multiverses originating from the Ninth Dimension. The Tenth Dimension contains non-physical space like the Ninth and has a non-polarity to it. The Ninth has a negative polarity and has s a downward pole toward the lower Eight Dimensions. The Eleventh Dimension has a positive polarity. The positive forces of Eleventh with negative polarities of the Ninth are in a state of balance in the Tenth in Sanskrit its - *Mulaprakriti – the mother of Mater and Energy*. Above the Eleventh Dimension, both Matter and Spirit do not exist.

The love of the high Lords of even higher Dimensions is there to correct our miscreated reality of the *One to Eight Dimensions* as being God's angelic forces, above our Eighth Dimension to bring love and joy to us as God's consideration for us here. In the Tenth Dimension, angels only start to co-create with God, but according to their own wills design for the lower life form or elsewhere; though, their divine logic creates bliss for the lower ones – namely us! Below the Tenth Dimension, its mathematical logic may be illogical in its design of which God can never put His name rightfully to it. God assists us anyway by blessing His offspring's every wish out of love regardless by blessing His Holy Spirit, but if it were up to Him, we would co-create with God otherwise according to His standards of logic. God was given us our free will by permitting us to try to understand Him foolheartedly by allowing us to miscreate to God's amusements.

I am sad to say that our branch of One to Eighth Dimensions, down with its uncountable number of Universes, are not Divine but personal self-deluded with logic that our source would not have derived as being sound. The literature of the east mentions the dreamlike false world of our mis creations as a world of pain and sufferings; it's the only way out is to understand and accept its pains.

To elaborate on my unique number theory, I state that all creation basic is on zero and the one binary system. From the start, the number *one* holds all infinity in a numeric value of *one*, a self-deluded concept. The number one is the source of all our self-deluded logical systems, which are falsely made to function by the grace of our source, whom we call God or the Lord.

The pre-existing state of our God and we have a numerical basic on the *negative zero – God,* and *positive zero – His infinite and eternal sons.* Only the negative zero of God can correct our mis creations – our known life as we experience it. Our positive zero self-ushered our mis creations in us as an attempt to get closer and to perfect our relationship with God; this is impossible as God gives us perfect love. Like the garden of Eden, we felt something was missing in our relationship with God. The apple eating shows that we misunderstood the perfect love God has for us – we questioned it!

Our multiverse is like a child painting the whites of the eyes in a *paint by numbers* purple, and the father laughs and says – "Perfect, my son/daughter."

God has His amusements over anything we come up with, like a three – four-year-old toddler talking nonsense with an infant's Mind to the delight of His father/mother. In other words, no matter how high you grow under the Eighth Dimensional set branch, we are still just a toddler talking nonsense to God. Our whole branch is like the children's board game 'Candy land," and God plays along with us to His amusement and laugher.

Now, let us consider other number theorists. I care to mention the three that had inspired me – Aristotle, Karl Gödel, and Giuseppe Peano.

The first: the number theory of Aristotle

In Aristotle's Posterior Analytics writings, he wrote about *three notions* crucial to His theory of scientific claiming that there are as a set: 'of every', 'per se' -kath' hauto - or 'in virtue of itself' and the universally - katholou. Although His exposition of these notions is tailored to His proofed theory, the notions are designed also to characterize the basic features of any scientific claim where the principal examples come mostly from mathematics.

A hold true 'of every' B if A holds of B in every case always. Note that this is a stronger condition than is meant in the Prior Analytics by 'A belongs to all B'. Mathematical example: point is on every line (i.e., every line has points on it). A=B as B=A. As A going to B is the same as B going to A.

A is per se with respect to B iff 'A' is in the account which gives the essence of B. Note that Aristotle does not say that A belongs to all B (e.g., 'nose' occurs in the definition to face, but 'having a mouth' does not belong to a face of a person), yet it is presupposed by the use Aristotle makes of it. Aristotle allows that there are immediate statements of the form, A belongs to no B. Mathematical examples: 'line' is in the definition of triangle, 'point' is in the definition of line. A= B of the most part only but not entirely, as B to A not entirely. Now, we are referring to a possible connection or association but also not taking upon it is another values A to B but be A along and B along.

A is per se1 with respect to B iff 'B' is in the account which gives the essence of A and A belongs to B. Mathematical examples: straight and circular arc belong to line, odd and even to a number. Some commentators have held that it is the disjunction which belongs per se2 (e.g., straight, or circular arc belongs per se_2 to all lines); others that the examples are that each predicate belongs per se_2 to the subject (e.g., straight belongs per se2 to (some) line). However, Aristotle writes know that not all lines are straight or circular. To say it simply: a connection to A to B is a connection regardless of it design.

A is per se2 iff 'A' indicates 'a this' (tode ti), i.e., 'A' refers to just what A is. At Post, Aristotle identifies the per se_3 with substance, the rock bottom of a syllogistic chain. However, one might well ask whether there must be an analogous notion within a science. If so, A would be per se3 if A is a basic entity in each science, an instance of the kind studied by the science. If so, the per se3 items in arithmetic would be units. To put it simply – A and B are both unique and apart from each other in its value or character.

A is per se4 with respect to B iff A belongs to B on account of A. Either no mathematical example is given, or the examples are - depending on how we read the text: straight or curved belongs to line and odd or even belongs to number, but these may be cases of per se2. The non-mathematical example is in getting its throat cut it dies in virtue of the throat cutting.

A belongs to B universally iff A belongs to all B and A belongs to B per se (in virtue of B) and qua itself (qua B). Here the notion of 'per se1' seems to be slightly different from those previously mentioned (it has been suggested that the sense is per se4), but, in any case, is said to be equivalent to 'qua itself'. Perhaps we need a fifth notion of per se.

B has/is A per se_5 (i.e., in virtue of B) iff A belongs to B qua B, i.e., there is no higher genus or kind C of B such that A belongs to C and so to B in virtue of belonging to C. Again, Aristotle does not mark out per se5 as a separate nation, so that the notion may be subsumed under per se4. Note that unlike per se1 and per se2, per se5 is in virtue of the subject of the predication.

Second theory: The Peano

Peano's Statements about equality; in modern treatments, these are often not taken as part of the Peano axioms, but rather as axioms of the underlying logic. The following three hypotheses are first-order statements about natural numbers expressing the fundamental properties of the successor operation; the ninth final axiom is a second-order statement of the principle of mathematical induction over natural numbers. An Italian mathematician and glottologist were a weak first-order system called Peano arithmetic Giuseppe Peano Italian: 27 August 1858. Peano is obtained by explicitly adding the addition and multiplication operation symbols and replacing the second-order induction axiom with a first-order axiom schema. 1. 0 is a natural number.

The following four hypotheses describe the equality relation. Since they are logically valid in first-order logic with equality, they are not considered part of "the Peano axioms" in modern treatments.

For every natural number x, $x = x$. That is, equality is reflexive.

1. For all natural numbers x and y, if $x = y$, then $y = x$. That is, equality is symmetric.
2. For all natural numbers x, y and z, if $x = y$ and $y = z$, then $x = z$. That is, equality is transitive.
3. For all a and b, if b is a natural number and $a = b$, then a is also a natural number. That is, the natural numbers are closed under equality.

4. The remaining axioms define the arithmetical properties of the natural numbers. The naturals are assumed to be closed under a single-valued "successor" function S.

5. For every natural number n, $S(n)$ is a natural number. That is, the natural numbers are closed under S.

6. For all natural numbers m and n, $m = n$ if and only if $S(m) = S(n)$. That is, S is an injection.

7. For every natural number n, $S(n) = 0$ is false. That is, there is no natural number whose successor is 0.

8. K and for every natural number n, n brings in K implies $S(n)$ is in K *then* K is contained in every number

The induction axiom is sometimes stated in the following form:

9 if φ is a unary predicate of such that: φ is true and for every natural number N, brings true implies that φ is true then φ n is true for every natural number of n.

Peano's original formulation of the axioms used 1 instead of 0 as the "first" natural number. This choice is arbitrary, as these axioms do not endow the constant 0 with any additional properties. However, because 0 is the additive identity in arithmetic, most modern formulations of the Peano axioms start from 0. Axioms 1, 6, 7, 8 define a unary representation of the intuitive notion of natural numbers: the number 1 can be defined as $S(0)$, 2 as $S(S(0))$, etc. However, considering the notion of natural numbers as being defined by these axioms, axioms 1, 6, 7, 8 do not imply that the successor function generates all the natural numbers different from 0. Put differently; they do not guarantee that every natural number other than zero must succeed some other natural number.

The intuitive notion that each natural number can be obtained by applying *successor* sufficiently often to zero requires an additional axiom sometimes called the *axiom of induction.*

Third theory: Gödel.

Kurt Friedrich Gödel, a German: April 28, 1906 – January 14, 1978) was a logician, mathematician, and analytic philosopher. Gödel is considered, along with Aristotle and Friedrich Ludwig Gottlob Frege, one of the most significant logicians in History; Gödel had an immense effect incompleteness theorem, which is a basis of mine.

The first incompleteness theorem states that no consistent system or Axion is a nanoparticle substance of the Universe. An Axion is an effective procedure, or to say, an algorithm of the Universe's life unseen by man but very evident to life itself. The capable of proving all truths regarding the art of algorithms noticed by natural numbers. There will always be statements about natural numbers that are true for any consistent formal system but unprovable within the system. The second incompleteness theorem, an extension of the first, shows that the system is not compatible. I have derived my number theorem, and I can't entirely agree with Gödel, but I find His thoughts as my basis. Now being that the Gödel number theorem is incomplete, I have mine as a supplement. Is mine final? It will be to future number theorists to amend it in time.

The system of math states its logic on negation, a logical complement of numbers. An operation that takes a proposition of {\displaystyle P} P to another proposition "not {\displaystyle P}P "Is interpreted intuitively as being true when {\displaystyle P}P is false, and false when {\displaystyle P}P is true. For example, an apple is true when the apple is wrong. Negation is thus a unary (single argument) logical connective. It may be applied as an operation on notions, propositions, truth values, or semantic values more generally. In classical logic, the negation is normally identified with the truth function that takes truth to falsity (and vice versa). In psychic reasoning research in accordance with the Brouwer–Heyting–Kolmogorov interpretation. The negation of a proposition {\displaystyle P} P is the proposition whose proofs is the refutations of P. In terms of God, He can only exist if there is no evidence of His existence at all. God is made real by not making His existence real at all. Woden in Norse mythology saw God as the invisible stranger or outside to all reality as we know it.

Last is mine – The Marcello theory

My theory is based on a more developed form of logic inspired by Gödel but original to Him in most aspects. It is called - negation, also called the logical complement. We have $X + (-0) / -X = +X$. The logic is that - 0 plus X is – 0 or God and us as the X God divined by the negative X or us equals X - us. Who is negative X? Negative X is God's beloved thoughts as His Song is a non-existing state. The fact rests that both God and we must be founded on a non-existing state to exist in the first place. Understandably, in my math system, (-0) is always paired with $(+ 0$ or to say $+ X)$, making the two equals to be X. The function is a differential, but of what? X, in this case, is projected as it is equal to infinity. The idea of the rate of any change to this function is projection $(-0) + (+ 0)$, or in other words, the relationship between God and His infinite Son. As far as infinity, the number one cannot sum up all infinity. We used to create all this fetched math as follows: the only way to understand numbers is to use my number theory to maintain a certain negative whole number to its possible outcome – a quasi-reality that we have come to accept as our reality.

Using $(- 3, -7, -11, -13 -17,$ and both $- 21, - 23)$ finally. This math most strongly uses -3, -7. We do have some use of -23, but it is less and less as you go on to a lower number.

* -3 ~ is the insult to what we call reality its challenges its validity by causing trouble to overcome.
* -5 ~ is the fact that our reality is false but conquering the uses of - 5 will create a near-perfect reality with - 0 only. This sums

up as -5 – 0 = 0, but equally – 5 or any other math may create beauty and purpose. It's almost impossible to use this, but only near godly agents can manage it. In the Thirteenth Dimension, you will understand it better. It's use makes the impossible made possible – in why our bodies work.

* -7 ~ is the manageable number that helps you create any for the rules and law in all mathematic of creation, but its powers are in its designed algorithmics. – 3 and -5 ae associated with – 7 got make your creation more manageable.

* -9 ~ is used to test your math at the end. Either is working, or not or never will.

* -11 ~ is a number that aids in making what you want easy with the - 0 if God. - 11 as a – a prove it - number. It causes you to verify your algorithm to the highest logic with God help and can validate if the algorithm right or will fail.

* -13 ~ offers possible clue to uncover in any math functionality with it results to your so-called reality.

* -17 ~ will stop you from using your math and causing you to think in a higher way. Only used it you are questioning reality apart from any number system. It is only working intuitively.

* -21 ~ is used but is needed in the long equation to moderate the math in its components required; it automatically streamlines the Algorithms.

* – 23 ~ is beyond any mathematician's abilities, but it can create life itself if it were used. Only higher developed life form can manage Understood in the Eighteenth Dimension only not before. True divinity is understood in its use and its successful management.

This math is for the *Demiurges/ Demi-gods Creative agent of God* to understand as Demiurges are the third manifestations of all things. They are not a single being, but rather the collectivity of all the creative powers of the cosmos which are guided by the abstract principle of Cosmic Ideation - or to say the *Mahat* or Divine though. The though is the primal idea of the First Dimension and expanded to all Thirty-three Dimensions by using number -23 in relationship with the rest. Only they can manage – 23 – no human can ever manage it or understand the algorithms that they use. Like others who came before me, my writings are inconclusive. In more advanced ages we expect updates to mine and the three above theories.

My only conclusion to this chapter of Number theory, concerning mine, is that God is the negative zero, and any number used after that is false. Our grand system of Multi Dimensions of uncountable Universes is all based on a false scenario in its design. God's Spirit came in our assistance and made it real enough for us to experience this false notion we have of God. He intends to make it a happy dream and for us, then to return to our sanity at one with Him. Yes, we can Mind's scope currently.

One good thing about this sad ending is that, as God is God, He holds us still with Him in our perfections in the negative 0 zero as co-creating wonders. We are unaware of this very fact, due to our minimal mental capacity currently.

Growth is possible in our third-Dimensional reality than others I cared to state now. Just to add an interesting fact, scientists found out that our seven universal cluster has three negatively polarized Universes to one side and three positively polarized one to the other side with a central Universe in the junction to the left and right groups three. Our whole universal cluster is blessed by the numerical value of seven in the Third Dimension.

The three theories are written by Aristotle, Peano, and Godel have been inspired by internet finds – both wiki and other website searches. Gödel's idea loosely inspires my theory, but my math is all original to my intuitive writing skills.

Chapter 5

What is a Dimension, Multiverse, Universe, and a Realm

What makes one Universe in our Multiverse special:

Our Universe has 300 million galaxies and two hundred trillion stars in the Universe; our Galaxy has one hundred billion stars. Scientists say that there might be twenty-four thousand Earthlike planets in our Galaxy alone and possibly three hundred million times in our Universe. Just how many inhabitable planets have intelligent life? If only ten percent, that is two thousand four hundred in our Galaxy alone. Referring to our Universe, apart from all other Universes in the uncountable Multiverse, one Universe apart from the rest must be unique and needed for personal growth and experiences; this raises the question! What makes out Universe under our One-to-Eight-Dimensional theme of 'Knowing God by trying to me Him' so unique? Well, in our Universal Cluster of seven Universes that we reside in, we are number four and in the positive arm of the Cluster. We, in turn, vibrate to a positive numerical value of the number four. So, we are dynamically structured then – but to do what? Well, there are many such Clusters like ours out there under our theme. So, what makes us stand apart? The difference is, in our Universe, we are masters at cooking food and creating a solitary home environment. Many in our Universe cooks in and talk to others outside of their homes rarely. We also enjoy entertaining friends in our homes, which is not seen much in other Universal Clusters. We do so in a dynamically structured way as the host in charge. We oversee our cooking in our kitchen and rule our solitude at home with many interested.

Yes, we like to go out and socialize too, but the home is our castle. In most of the universal life in other Clusters, a whole town would live in a common area setting with very little privacy. The Norse Icelandic people did this in the winter months. The entire community would live in a large house. They must have lived like a house of cats, sharing the space, but staking off their territories for some sense of privacy.

I feel that planetary life in other Universal Clusters is much more affectionate than planetary life in our Cluster. We live in a dynamic Universe, which makes planetary life warmer given stagnate Universe in our Cluster. We seem to relish our privacy in our Universe. We are like this because we are befriending and knowing ourselves. Nowhere else in the vast majority of Universes are their masters in the kitchen like we are. You can go to any Universes in our Cluster of any numerical value and find that cook does not want anyone in their kitchens but alone. We are masters of cooking, homemaking in our Cluster of seven Universes and very much in charge in our Universe at home and in the kitchen. As you can see, what makes a Universal Cluster and a particular Universe different from others may seem to us as ridiculous and unimportant; but in the larger picture, it makes a world of difference to the Jiva – soul-seeking experience in incarnating.

What might be the experience in other Universal Clusters? Who is to say, but one thing I can say is not to laugh at their differences from us? What seems ever so insignificant to one Cluster may be necessary to others in the long run. In one Cluster, outdoor social life might be the thing, and home life barely exists. In another, one's career might be all that is needed at home and social is neglected. In one Custer, their happiness comes from the external, and inner happiness needs to be learned. I am just guessing, though, am I can be right too?

I do make three words of advice now:

1. For us to be the masters of our kitchen by taking up cooking. We can take classes or study cookbooks and learn the techniques of good cooking and cleaning as we cook our food. Learn the tools and equipment required for our special dish too.

2. For us to live in our perfect dream home with furniture and decoration that reflects our character. I also suggest we take up many interests and hobbies besides watching television. Learn an instrument or take up writing or Art. I play the Harp, Piano, and Violin quite well. I am currently learning how to compose Piano and Harp sheet music. Oh yes, I enjoy writing and editing my works, as we can see.

3. For us to be the host of a party in our lovely homes and set a warm atmosphere of love and joy. Bad associations only disrespect the inner God of who we are; it took me many years to learn this valuable. Fact – it's better to be alone than unhappy! We have a God-given right to be loved and have our happiness. Proper behavior protects us from harmful consequences that usually come through others.

So, we must cook up a storm, design our dream home and be with loved ones in our house occasionally. Overall, be friends with us first!

1 – What is a Dimension? - width, depth, and height are Dimensions. For example, a cube has three Dimensions. Physics can also mean any physical measurement such as length, time, mass, etc. A Dimension locates a position in space. A Dimension is not a natural concept because Dimensions do not exist in nature. Instead, Dimensions were devised to refer to locations. They are referrals, not referents. In other referrals include maps, distances, dates, numbers, and money. Each of the referrals are meant to provide a set of values in which measurements can be made.

This reference is the definition of a frame of reference as Dimensions. One Dimension locates a line. So, the Dimension is not the line but a reference for the line. Again, the Dimension is not a natural concept but a referral for lines. It is an artificial concept. Written in some texts, Dimensions are treated as natural concepts and have properties and causes; this is not true. Dimensions are only frames of reference and consequently have no properties or cause other than as referrals. The size of a living Dimension is 10 ^-33. The rule is: it gets larger the smaller it seems to us. A live Dimension is far smaller than 10^-33? As it is much larger than that.

A living Dimension lies on the surface of the higher Dimension and is bent like a sphere. Our Third Dimension is like a film with many cells to create an illusion of a three-Dimension particular form two Dimensional cells. Our time here actually seems to run forward, but subconsciously in runs backward, and so is the opposite in the Seventh Dimension. Time in our Dimension is truly backward linear time. However, we have fourth-Dimensional poles of our planet, which does create nonlinear time to be used by our higher Minds for our growth here.

Other planets in our Universe rarely have such a fourth-Dimensional polarity; this accelerates our growth here as designed by our Earth mother so we can evolve and leave her alone. The Earth mother of our Yellow Realm prefers to host only microbial life, insect, animal, fish, and birdlife only – no intellectual life as we are, however.

I capitalize the word Dimension as is spoken in terms of being a non – a place in my writing. I do not use capitulation to describe the Dimension as Dimensional – an adjective, only a noun is capitalized. Both the words Multiverse and Realms are a proper space/object as well used in my writings. The words spirit and soul are not capitalized, but Master Soul and master Spirit indicate a finished result.

The locations of various Dimensions are both on a third and seventh-Dimensional membrane on the larger scheme of all Dimensions as a whole. The reason why the Third and Seventh Dimensions are marks is in their uses of time. The Third Dimension uses positive sequential time, even though time is running subconsciously backward, while the Seventh Dimension uses negative sequential time thought subconsciously running forward.

A New Aged book I read many years ago mentions that all time had already happed, and the past is the only tangible form of time. We are currently unknown to us subconsciously; we are in a retrograde mode to examine it all to understand what a ridiculous theme we have in our set of One to Eight Dimension and only to leave it. Our Master Spirit employs such a device of time, and with even higher Lord help us leave this bad dream we are in at any given moment and return to sanity and be with our God insanity.

In the Seventh Dimension, it is in reverse. Time goes backward to view the future of us at one with our source – God. This odd concept of time is impossible to comprehend, being that we cannot experience it ourselves. The idea of the Seventh in terms of time – is to reach the original cause of the fall from God's side to this odd and horrible dream we are located. The point of causation is far more apparent there, so awakenings to your God nature are easier. We, in our Dimension are running away from our enlightenment to God. We only subconsciously have spiritual awareness.

That is why I feel that the conscious Mind education of God is ridiculous. All those Seminary schools and Temple training are a joke. Our dreams are the best way to study spirituality. Keep a dream journal and ask questions for answers to be revealed at night. One more other way is to do creative writings and poetry with a loving, open heart.

2- What is a Multiverse? - Quantum Physicist says that $10^{10^{500}}$ Universes make up a Multiverse. That is not to say there are more and different Multiverses in other Dimensions. I feel that number is referring to our Dimension alone. A Multiverse is many Universes far away from one and another. They all exist in a vacuum apart from each other. It is impossible to view other Universes, even if you might be on the outer edge of a Universe; light cannot travel in a vacuum. The nature of a Universe is, no matter where you are in a Universe, you are at its center. Not in its true center, but the center in respect to our travels; this makes traveling to our Universes edge impossible. These Universes are clustered in groups of a set number value. In our Dimension, they can only be in a set of one, two, three, four, five, six, seven, eight. Our universal cluster possesses seven Universes.

Each Universe has its own laws of physic that rules life there. One has a unique experience range there that other Universes cannot offer. One chooses a particular Universe or cluster to suite their unique experiences required. Yes, there are soul groups, and the decision to move on to new Universe are made amongst the group's members. The choices of experience for a group to decide is overwhelming to consider. Choosing one Universe out of 10^{500} is beyond any humans of Mind. The selection of experiences it like being at a buffet with 10^{500} foods to choose from – impossible. I feel that our eight-Dimensional Thought Adjuster can only make such a choice for our group or us.

Each Universe has its own soul body to help itself inhabitance grow according to its chosen lessons and experiences required of their Monads. Our universal soul's body is called – Sophia! She is the goddess of wisdom in the Gnostic Faith. Her nature is passive, being female. Our group of seven Universes is a seven sister's cluster. We, thus, have a doubly passive, receptive Universe. However, our Universe rests on the active/positive branch of our universal cluster. So, we can reflect our universal cluster theme of growth and required experience in an active manner and reflect the larger width and scope of all other cluster's main themes to a small degree. The other clusters are of a third Dimensional multi-Realm consciousness. Though, primarily to our Yellow Realm, but respective to all Realms of the Third's consciousness.

3 – What is a Realm? - A Realm is a subdivision of a Dimension. For example, we have seven subdivisions in our Dimension. In an individual Realm – all one can see in their visible Universe is that Realm itself. The higher lords called the Demiurges – *creative lord* devised this mathematical algorithm for our Dimension of having Seven Realms based on one primary color added to each. We have mixed colors, too, a making seven-colored Realms in our Third Dimension. Each Realm is influenced by its Color vibrations. There is a higher Dimension with colors unseen by humans in our reality here. The Seventh Dimension has Seven primary colors; this makes Seven physical Realms and Seven energetic Realms in the Seventh Dimension. The Fourth Dimension has four physical Realms and four energetic – astral Realm. Each Realm is a reality. Their visible Universe is of the Realm alone. I care to go back to the $10\text{\textasciicircum}10\text{\textasciicircum}500$ numerical value of Universes – is that referring to our yellow Realm alone? Or the whole fold of three other Realms plus our semi-physical purple Realm? Hum? Who is to say?

The First Dimension has only one Realm, the Second Dimension three Realms, including a semi-physical/energetic Realm. The Third Dimension – us- has seven Realms, the Fourth Dimension has nine Realm, the Fifth Dimension has eleven Realm, the Sixth Dimension has thirteen Realms, and finally, the Seventh Dimension has seventeen Realms. This math system used a rainbow. Interestingly, a rainbow has seventeen colors in the Seventh Dimension – now that is a huge rainbow!

3.1 Physical Realms - The physical is unique in that it infuses sweet atoms into all souls for their growth; this is impossible in the Astral energetic Realms. Sweet atoms are the key to growth in an expanding

Universe. The more the Universe expands, the more souls expand too. This expansion includes all living life, both seen and unseen; both considered small or large; and both important and unimportant to man's reasoning. Only in the physical Realms can one grow by sweet atoms.

3.2 Energetic Realms - Sweet atoms projects inner expansions of the soul for its growth. In the Astral Realm, one validated their growth by being a particular part of society in that Realm. They perform such duties until the hunger for sweet atoms is overwhelmingly required. They then plan an incarnation to a physical Realm to acquire such sweet atoms. Yes, the more industrious upon the Earth acquires more sweet atoms; the less industrious only acquire enough to maintain their physical structure. Some New Aged books write that the Green Realm, our Astral, above our Yellow Realm is where future souls come to incarnate to the Earth and where we go after death. The book mentions that our Earth's Green Realm is like a village, with the Earth being just a house. The book is trying to say that a majority of souls live in the Green Realm. Some souls only return to Earth to renew their bodies and regain youth in the Green Realm alone. They need to rest in such an environment to plan higher lives elsewhere in the Universe or other Realm. Our Astral is the heart chakra of our Dimension and is the most populated Realm for souls to dwell. We will speak on the importance of the Yellow Realm we are in currently in a coming chapter.

3.3 What is Sweet Atoms? – Sweet Atoms are the enrichments of the ever-expanding Universe. Sweet Atoms feed the souls in the energetic-Astral Realm directly. Such feeding in the Astral does not foster growth but maintains life. It does not maintain life in the physical, but it is the key to applying self-work proper growth in both Realm of the physical and energetic. No real growth occurs in energetic Realms, but only in physical Realms. Sweet Atoms can only be infused with a soul in the physical Realm alone. Sweet Atoms are the life of the Universe and its soul's entity itself. Here in our Yellow Realm, we must grow one a one-to-one level with the universal soul, which is, in our case – yellow. Yellow vibrations encouraged the Mind and the joy of life. We have s tight connection with our thought Adjuster here in our Realm for the best choices in life for us to make.

4- What is a Universe? These Universes are clustered in groups of any basic number value. In our Dimension, they can only be in a set of one, two, three, four, five, six, seven, eight. Our universal cluster possesses seven Universes.

Each Universe has its laws of physic that rule life there; One has a unique experience range there that other Universes cannot offer; One chooses a particular Universe or cluster to suit the unique experiences required. Yes, there are soul groups, and the decision to move on to a new Universe is made amongst the group's soul members. The choices of experience for a group to decide on being overwhelming to consider. Choosing one Universe out of $10\wedge10\wedge500$ is beyond any human of Mind. The selection of experiences is like being at a buffet with $10\wedge10\wedge500$ foods to choose from – impossible. I feel that our eight-Dimensional Thought Adjuster can only make such a choice for our group or us. Our Universe I named – Sophia – the Gnostic Goddess of Wisdom. I wrote about her in the seventh chapter – please read on!

Chapter 6

Dimensions One to Eight The many names of God

In Dimension One to Eight we find ourselves in the Physical/ Energetic. I shall elaborate on the Physical/Energetic, or earthly, and spiritual now for our understanding of how we get deeply involved in our personal relationships in our physical/energetic realities for their highest rewards. God may use us as co-creator to gain experience in various Universes of inhabits in an attempt of God to heal us from the bad dream we befell ourselves. This Attempt is the God assist self-help for us. He has a focus to us here in healing this bad dream we made apart from His wholeness. You might ask then: What is the Physical/Energy, and why does not God approve of it?

The Physical: The Physical is not the opposite of the spiritual as the Christian Scientist preaches. What we call the spiritual has a significant number of physical properties in its complexities. Many spend a lot of time in its worlds of wonder, the inhabitants of the Spiritual/Energetic planes we incarnate. They may respond quite physically to their environment and their neighbors as they may do here upon our Earth. However, in such semi - Energetic/Physical Realms (the spiritual), there are vast differences compared to our Realm of Earth.

The technologies in their spiritual Realms are interwoven in their DNA and organs of their inhabitance. They can think of a particular location in their planes or other spiritual planes and be there in a split second. They can communicate mutually in a telepathic manner – Mind to Mind; they don't grow old and die, but they do need to incarnate to the physical Realms of their associated multiverse in their associated, unique Dimensions of Multiverse. For example, our *Third Dimension's Yellow Realm renews* their Astral bodies and opens themselves to their higher experiences. This exercise is a requirement as the infused energies given by our Universal expansion rest in the truly Physical - sweet atom of the physical and no semi-physical Universe.

What is the Physical is another form of the Energetic, but compressed in an ordered and designed manner? Of such, its behavior and benefit apart from the Energetic is in opposition as in Stagnate/Physical – Earthly; and Dynamic/Energetic – the Spiritual Realms. The Physical has a grounding, stabilizing, and housing benefit to it. Clearly, the Physical is not entirely physical like the Energetic/Spiritual is not entirely Energetic.

How is the Physical necessary for growth in the Spiritual/Energetic? The answer is – Sweet atoms! Sweet atoms are Earth Mother type atoms that foster life and growth by transmitting Spirit/Energetic into the Matter/Physical causing – sweet atoms. These sweet atoms infuse in the incarnate and build up a treasure to expand upon in one's afterlife in the Spiritual/Energetic and Physical existences alike. One may rebuild an unworkable physical body used to incarnate into the Physical Realms or build upon whom he/she may be and where he/she wants to evolve both physically and spiritually. The transmutation of the Physical to the Spiritual in one's body gives the result of sweet atoms. In the flesh, we call to the spirits of the energetic Realms automatic for help, thus inviting such power to enter us for our growth. This spiritual helper channels the infused energies from the universal expansion toward us from our Physical Realm.

What is the Dynamic? In our Realm, it's Ions and Gravitons. In the larger Universe, it is that plus Dark Energy. Dark Energy consists of 68 percent of our Universal volume. It expands our Universe at an accelerated rate. The ratio of Matter and Dark Matter of Dark Energy is very close to roughly 2.33, which is the acceleration rate of the Universe. The five others (physical to semi-physical Realms) with our Yellow Realm are only thirty percent of all Matter, with roughly twenty-five percent being our associated other Realms parallel and internal to our Yellow Realm - of the Minds. Other Dimensions have no presence in the larger sense, but only in the microscopic sense that is undetectable and only sense of inner atomic research.

So, is Dark Matter, Spirit? No! What we call Spirit interacts in the Dark matter Realm of souls with some outside help from higher Dimensions. The greater Dimensional influence toward us is subatomic, leaving the Dark Matter's Realm to influence us directly. So, as a fact, Dark Energy houses both Master and Dark Matter like Dark Mater houses our mother. Dark Energy is present as the living force of both mother/Dark Matter. So, why does it seem to destroy our Universe with its expansion rate of 2.33? Well, if it did not behave in such a manner, its life-forces would not be infused in both Dark and Light Matter. Quantum physics has not yet come up with this in a mathematical formula. I state now that both living infusions of both Matter and its expansion are the same, roughly 2.33. As it destroys Matter, it infuses it with life. This life/death story is common in astrophysics. Yes, the speed of the Universe's expansion, progress, and evolution are the same. In the early days of our Universe, seventeen billion Earth years ago, all progress was relatively slow. Personal happiness and trying to be who we are being difficult in the earlier years of our Universe. Now, improvement is relatively fast and will accelerate even more in the future until all ends in a frenzy of joy! If you feel that the next place you will go after this world is "Heaven," you are wrong! The closest Dimension to anything that comes close to "Heaven" is a Seventh Dimensional higher gas-like Realms. Suppose you are a Jehovah's Witness and believe in their new system in a paradise Earth. In that case, you might need to gain a Seventh-Dimensional orientation toward it and incarnate there as life evolves onward. You will be likely in that Seventh Dimensions lower physical. However, the Jehovah's Witnesses are self-deluded in their belief that they will live forever in a human body in such a paradise planet with a superior entity that they call their Jehovah God from a higher Realm to rule over them.

What is an Astral? An Astral is not made up of free form energy from the physical Realms but responds the both the physical lower to it and higher. An Astral is like a mirror to both physical Realms but is independent and of an element in its own both at the same time. An Astral is a Realm of rest and expansions of the soul and needed for growth and education for future physical lives.

I will delineate an outline of the set of eight Gods named Dimensions now: The First Dimension is ethical archetypical and archetypical of the founding word of how we view God. Our First Dimensional theme is – to know God; we much try to be God ourselves. This Dimension's understanding is the point that is nowhere but everywhere at the same time. In this Dimension, all points and lines stand apart from the rest as being valid, though all are equally valid. All life there is seen as the only one alone, but not exclusively the whole and complete with respect to other lives there in its group soul formation.

The Second Dimension is Semi-physical/Energetic and is the foundation of all other Dimensions in their directions to follow using its two vectors. The Duality of follow through with one's intent or returning to its source is present there. Many do return to the Divine after knowing the insanity of what is ahead of them. The return identifies as good, and the bad identifies as continuing to higher Dimensions with its associated multiverses; this makes all other sequential Dimensions of the multiverse bad but houses the chance for them to return to their source, as well. For those who have chosen to follow, though, they plan out all lines everywhere in all Dimensions with the Eighth-Dimensional Demiurges – Creators, overseen by even higher lords. This Dimension only has three Realms – white, black, and grey.

The Third Dimension – The Dimension of recognition and extraordinary love. Here, we have three vectors: X-left/right; Y -up/down; and Z- front/back; this creates our Third-Dimensional Realm. Recognition and specials of manifesting the Godman are known here. We live in round Planets and Suns and disk-like Galaxies in a round spherical Universe – all three Dimensional. One can do not go back in time here short of their Minds. We have four Physical Realms with three Spiritual/Energetic Realms to live and evolve. This Dimension has seven Realms – Red, Yellow, Blue are Physical; Green, Orange is semi-physical and Spiritual/Energetic. The Purple Realm is a unique brand of Spirit/matter hard to explain but can respond as physical and spiritual at the same time. Their internal forms balance between the two. The Mind and intentions of their inhabitance may dictate the outcome to be physical or spiritual, depending on their needs. Shambhala is there; it is spiritual but does have a physical location over the Himalayas in Tibet.

The Fourth Dimension – The Dimension of the lords of compassion. Its vectors are as above but with one more – inside/outside. The planets, Suns, Stars, Galaxies, and their Universe are still like the Third but houses an emerging double that inducts the external in a cycle of death and renewal. One's time indicates from its beginning to its end is like a snake, but only appears in time if focused on its choice timeline. One can time travel in the Fourth and choose to correct a shortsighted choice. In that event, they can travel back in time and choose better. However, such a change of destiny would nearly cancel their previous timeline destiny for a new one. Such change would alter all inter-reactions of the old future to passive chance. These inter-reactions would be retained in all who were involved as a reduction in passive inter-reacts only. One some sense, the old destiny line will happen, but not holding such to the new one or those involved. True love and compassion are seen there as one's unknown self is revolved. One's unknown aspects of Him/herself are visible to all. One can truly get to know their unknown selves there and others know them alike. Many lords of compassion serve as an angel from there to help us, humans, here. The Hindu faith calls that Dimension Heaven or, in Sanskrit - Nirvana!

The Fifth Dimension - the soul twin, soul mates Dimension! In this Dimension, we have the same vectors as the fourth, but one more vector – You/Me; or to say, the whole set of the Fourth projects in multiples as aspects of the first projection. Time travel is more liberal compared to the Fourth Dimension. One does not have to return to the point of choosing again to direct tone destiny differently. A Fifth Dimensional soul can directly meet its new self in another timeline destiny. The old destiny would continue at the same time as the new destiny. Both destinies will identify as the same soul but free to express themselves in a multi-faceted manner of Him/her/itself. In this Dimension, you encounter your past existences as different people to inter-react with and get to know; this is an energetic ethereal Dimension and does not follow traditional physical pacific rulings. Everything in this Dimension is Mind projected. One can even relive alternative possibilities of misunderstood events in one's hurt or puzzling past. In this Dimension, you genuinely get to know yourself. One works with their Karm directly to system and organize it to the Universal law of fine growth. Not all alien races can grow to a higher Dimension if unlawful; by no chance the Fifth.

The Sixth Dimension - The many souls Dimension. One is fractured into many souls that embody both new, different destinies and interests in this Dimension. The vector is like the Fifth, but with a new vector to add to – of *Inner Duality* or *contrary states of beings;* this is the denial of who we think we are entirely as it opens us up to states of being totally outside of our scope of past experiences. A higher force fractures us beyond our scope of Mind; unlike in the Fifth, where the fracturing was in our range of Mind, this is beyond our Minds scope here. Time travel is more liberal three before it. One can manifest as a different soul entirely in an associated different Universe to live out their new choice. One will have absolutely nor holding to the old soul at all. This Sixth Dimension has a Third-Dimension polarity, so we are projected to new destinies as new souls in new multiverses in the lower Dimension but more likely in the Third Dimension. Strange dreams can be awakened there to reality if the forces are high enough.

The Seventh Dimension – The Dimension of the perfected soul! The new vectors(direction) here, to add, is – *the God direction!* This God vector is unique to the individual and is the union of all multi-souls coming from the Sixth Dimension. One is a unique *Godman-made manifested.* In this Dimension of many Realms, one first gets in touch with God. They are *sons of God* like Saint Michael, *who knows God;* this is the Dimension of the Hebrew and Christian Archangels mentioned in the Bible. They reach humanity to offer a Godly sense of orientation. The buoyancy there is very difficult to maintain. The need to incarnate to lower Dimensions of multiverses of multi-Realms are obliged there. Many times, souls living there would be asked to serve in lower domains. They do have their free will, but they would be forced to serve if they disobeyed for long. With Godlike abilities there, any form of time travel is arranged without complication, and it is pretty direct.

The Eighth Dimension - This is the Dimension of our name of God? Our human reach of Mind limit is under this eighth Dimensional hold. Our God name we chose there is – *getting to know God by trying to be Him.* This name echoes in all experiences in the First to Eighth Dimensions. The newly added vector here is – is a semi-real sense of infinity! The vector is in the question of going to the infinite or the finite; its purpose here is to establish itself as infinite as possible to unite itself with the Divine, which happened to be truly infinite. All its self-validation of its reality rests upon this false notion. This false notion and its God name are maintained here to stabilize this set of Eighth Dimensions; this is a nonphysical Dimension. The souls who live there are masters at transforming both matter and spirit- the physical and energy to their likings. Both states of matter and spirit are interchangeable, there and known as one state. I can only allude to this state as being the state of Mind.

What does each *set of One to Eight* all have in common? What sets them apart from other sets of One to Eights; and what does that mean regarding our growth here and now? The answer is simple – to try to get to know God by trying to be Him ourselves is our chosen ruddle for us now, and other sets of One to Eight have their uniquely own riddle to answer in coming to know God better. Practically, all can revolve around us as we are being Gods ourselves. One false notion that cannot help but enter is that we killed God in trying to be God Himself; this allows all – so-called evil and guilt to be a part of our world and life here. Both self-consciousness and evil go hand and hand. The guilt we feel about God, not being present here is evidence enough for us that we did kill Him to gain our self-consciousness – Live. We overlook the sense memory of God here - His Holy Spirit. It is impossible to avoid evil in our Universe. Evil is even in advanced alien life on their planets. They handle such evil more efficiently than we do, but there are some breeds of aggressive aliens. There is a ring of supporting alien life to protect us here, though. We need not worry.

In each of the listed Dimensions, the Multiverse is full of numerous Universes with numerous planetary cultures; they have the central characteristics to its Dimensions in common, but with a vast difference between them in each Universe and planetary civilization. I care not to generalize a particular Dimension as there is a vast difference in our Universe, for example. Still, there remain many familiar treats that we all share in our own Universe and Dimension.

I close my thoughts on this set of Eight by reminding my readers that we are in the Third Dimension, and that special love and recognition from others are fine here. So, have that special love and be rich and famous – it is forgivable appropriate here! We do have a Fourth-Dimension polarity here to confuse us, though. The closing part of the Third-Dimension chapter covers these issues and our polarity with the Fourth Dimension.

Chapter 7

Dimension Zero and the First

I n the Kabbalah we see the Ain Soph Aour. Ain is nothingness; Soph is infinity; Aour is light or life. Before we were, and the Dimensions were, there was nothingness. There the kabbalah agrees with my writings. The Kabbalah was its origins in Egypt. Its symbol of the Ankh. The Jew learned this system while in Egypt in the Delta. Hebrew angels and names were replaced from Egyptian names and gods/goddesses. The major arcana in the Tarot deck is Egyptian.

In my writings I state: We have fallen into this dream of separation from our source – God to try to be Him as much as possible to know Him better; this was affirmed in our First Dimensional state as a group entity – to be God Himself! We found no other way to adore, love, and know our source in any other way but to try to be Him ourselves. As the life force enters the First Dimension, it becomes a Monad – the first and single form of life with no beginning or end. A Monad is a Divinity in a dot! It is all things but all things to itself at the same time. In its journey into higher Dimensions, the Monad remains as the soul's life force. In union with Source – God, the Monad becomes a drop in the sea of all life to be the sea. The sea is God's body. One becomes of God's body but not God Himself, which is impossible.

Referring to creation, The Aeon – *glory of God expressed in creation,* of the Monad, our original intention of creating our set of *One to the Thirty-third Dimensions* was to do just that – to be God Himself *self-glorified.* One of our many souls cannot do this feat singly in the Sixth Dimension, or spirits cannot do this feat singly in Ninth Dimension in trying to be God Himself. This feat may not happen until the perfect spirit develops its will in trying to create an alternative self-made deluded Godhead in realities for lower life forms to use; this is the result of its failure in trying to be God Himself.

In a New Age self-help book called: A course in miracles, the text says that we killed God to have our independent egoist-consciousness. The book also wrote that due to that, we felt that God would punish us as guilty in our subconscious runaway thinking we falsely possess. This idea might be the self-deluded source of the evil we find in relationships and the world – ghostly phantom we call evil spirits. Its agents of this self-made evil are in archetype, as the devil, Satan, demons, ghouls, etc., of which are all forces of nature and not embodied with soul – or to say, truly living. Those forces of evil are in our illogical math set up in creating our Dimensions of One to Twelve. This mathematical algorithm's correction is over the Dimensions in the twenties where we are outside of the self and open to God interventions in its logic used.

The First Dimension
(All is one – or is it?)

The one point with no direction – the infinite finite. The pressure of being all things but just one thing alone. Vector: none. Like the illusion of the Eighth Dimension of not being INFINITE, so is the First Dimension - as *All* or, to say, INFINITE as FINITE at the same time; This is true but of solely on the imaginary p – possibilities and i – the amount of ps. Might you want to jump ahead to Chapter Eight's explanation of this illusive INFINITY? You will get a better idea of its nature. The fact is, there are many Ones - Dimensions of sets of *one to eight* Dimensions of God names under the Ninth Dimension and so true with what we call – *these sets of ninth Dimension sets of uncountable set* under the Tenth Dimension. The truth about infinity is that it's a tube one travels around on. By the time we get back to our starting point, all multiverses died and were reborn differently and not to be recognized. Our Dimensions are like a tube. The Dimension after the 321st is the First Dimension on the high end as Dimensions go up, then down, they go. If on the low end when 321st is low, Dimensions go up. The only difference is that up-first Dimensions go down and are passive when low-First Dimensions are active. They are going up and down simultaneously in different multi-branches; our branch is downward and passive. Life is emphatic in passive branches. In active branches, one needs to do to be and not just be to do. The First Dimension is a blank to start with, so all seems new but old.

Mysteriously, leaving not one *set or set of sets* to claim that there rest alone *one absolute real* set or set of sets to be deemed real in God's eyes. How can we explain the riddle of how finite realities can be infinity: They are all finite to their infinite possibilities as Universes dead and are reborn again? Souls are entering them and leaving them from the truly divine, and unquestionably, these sons of God have an infinite nature in blessing these sets with their divine nature. These two conditions: endless rebirths of universes and blessings from the Divine as sons of God enter and leave the sets, makes such set of one-to-eight-Dimension infinite enough to function as so-called infinite. Those wonderful Jives - *souls that incarnate to gain experience* - go into these multi-Dimensional multiverses and return to the Divine who creates a sense of all-ness and infinity in it, seeking out of its infinite possibilities of experience in these set of sets of One to Eight Dimensions.

One might think that this one, like in the First Dimension where our starting point is Javas, when in fact, they are backward projections of the so-called infinite Eight Dimensions. Such Multi-Eights, in turn, project their Eighth to First Dimensions out from the Ninth Dimension in branches into uncountable scopes of Mind of the creations of the multiverse, in like manner, uncountable First Dimensions of different versions of original God themes expressed as a one-ness to work out its riddle or to leave it behind is arranged. If I were to indicate any of the many First Dimensions in question, I would be false isolating that one to be apart from the rest. For that fact, being that there are uncountable First Dimensions, what First Dimension am I referring to anyway? Just because I state it as the first Dimension, that doesn't mean that another First Dimension of All-ness exists.

So, the question remains, is the one true one alone? No! There is potential in imaginary numbers of those up. I, an infinite amount of First Dimension with the unique concept of its sense of Oneness – God themes - accredited to an understanding God in question. "i "being an imaginary number, or to say, the amount and "p" potential of question regarding our God to understand our source. The "i" and "p" are crucial to all higher math in "calculus", "statistic and probabilities," "linear algebra," and "quantum physics." I feel intuitive that even higher math than quantum will take us much farther, but one more than even that will bring us to the level of math used by advanced alien life forms in advanced cultures used in their planets. Our math is still relatively primitive currently. I hope my math theorem might be helpful by its use of negative numbers with negative zero.

How do you describe oneness? Each person may have an idea of what oneness is. Can I say that all souls are at one with no differences of opinions of what oneness is? The answer is No. It is by virtue that, in our state of oneness, you carry states from Dimensions of the one to the Eighth that holds a unified concept of what oneness means to us.

Moreover, it holds us unique unified as we need to question God's nature; This raises the question of being of a different set of One to Eight with a different God question? Yes, to some degree, this is so, but our focus is our current question to the riddle of God nature tout current set of One to Eight. Our current question of God's nature is to our set - to understand God by trying to be God Himself. Our associated another riddle/question might be Is God a lie? We might have multiple riddles of God, nature to answer, but currently hold fast to the main one; this fosters unique individuality.

The death of individuality is in the Thirteenth Dimension, and its awakening to the My *God will be known* - body. A state of the Nine to Twelve does hold its originality and self-growth, but to try to explain it is beyond my human brain's scope or consciousness to depict as the Mind stops in the Eight Dimension, therefore, leaving a disadvantage in its explanation. However, I do have writing attempting to try to illustrate those Realms as much as possible. They practice the Arts, Music, and Drama that goes beyond the Human Mind's understandings.

Mulapakriti is in balance, in the Eleventh Dimension between negative Mulapakriti in the Tenth and positive Mulapakriti in the Twelve deals with such Arts. Music and Drama with a vehicle beyond the human Mind in its expressions and manifestation here. Mulapakriti is the mother of all matter and energy. The Chapter of the Ninth to Twelve Dimensions will cover this topic. The Ninth Dimension is unique because it balances the lower eight sets of Dimensions with their associated multiverses to Mulapakriti of the Tenth to the Twelfth Dimensions. The Ninth Dimension's role will cover this topic in the last quarter of that Chapter Nine.

The use of what we call Mind stops in the Eighth Dimension, and our Egoist self-consciousness stops the Twelve Dimension. What is truly infinity can only be experienced in the Thirteenth Dimensions. The First and the Twelve Dimensions are co-joint in their self-validation of infinity. Any concept of divinity can be considered valid and cannot be dismissed apart from the rest. Our so-called creations of the Divine come from God being entertained by such concepts and embracing them, even if false.

God's passive ways are glimpsed in the Tao Te Ching. One poem state that God is not a great and mighty mountain, but the lower valley as it can receive all waters and house all that comes. In the Tao, words that cannot be spoken are the only true words. Anything that can be explained in words is based on the author's impressions and subject to the author's personality. I said it before, any so-called words of God are fictional and only for the naïve and gullible. These people are too shallow not to search for the realities of life and their inner Truth within. They attract religions to teach them about God and tell them how to behave and believe. These faiths only keep them shallow and conservative in fear of looking to the unknown within them all. Oh, yes! That external source has the answers; now I don't have to look within me, they say – easy, right!

True life has a lustful and unpredictable nature to it. The Truth of love is beyond the author's human brain to conceptualize using words and can only mislead us, though many try to use poetry and art to achieve it at their best. In our Third-Dimension love is shaded with specials and a need for recognition. For all sacks and purposes, we need to be appreciated to our Dimension. Earth has a dual association to a Third- and Fourth-Dimension polarity for some odd reason; This makes us unique apart from our alien neighbors nearby who only have a Third Dimensional polarity. As a result, we love searches for the compassion of our inner being to be nurtured and recognized. I also mentioned in my writings that the highest form of lovelies is one's creativity. Such passion is individual and illogical to others. One may ask: Why does he play His violin all day long? True Godly passion may be seen as insanity to many, but divine to the player. Who is to judge one insane passion? They are of the insane logic of God, which is unknowable and futile to question. So, accept it all as the mysteries of life itself and do not question others' passions – now this is true maturity!

So, is there any truth to God in validating a unique oneness in any of the uncountable First Dimensional states? How can it be described that there can be multiples of the one? The Truth is, it is all arbitrary and God allows all those no-sense ideas accredit to Him by His sons out of love and laughter; and they all are the aspect of each other as if they were all one but different shades of the one. The undiscovered implication of negative zero makes it all work and evolve to its best beyond our awareness. God as *negative 0* is my addition to the current day metaphysics. Can one explain negative 0. No, not nothing but *negative nothing* or to say all things of having and being is beyond our limits of the Mind. We as *positive 0* are nothing or, to declare, *the void*, but we balance negative 0 in all to realize it by negative zero - God. Thus, we are the awareness of God in His infinite possibilities of creations and experiences of the imaginations. This unknown fact about all life is the key to all existence everywhere.

The Hua Hu Ching writes that any name or description of God is all false, fetched, and fictitious. Each state of oneness is one word of a collected depiction of what we feel God is with us. The many names of God are infinite. So too are the states of oneness with their branches from the First to the Eighth Dimensions with the many sets of One to Eights under the Ninth Dimension are.

We elected to identify with a chosen state of oneness - according to it, the concept of God, it holds as a group soul, and we entered it as Jives. Our chosen word of God is: To understand God by trying to be God Himself. In the Second Dimension, we gain our individual bodies to celebrate our departure for a group soul of the First Dimension. Now, in the Third Dimension, to gain unique ego-based recognition and self-identify using many ages lives.

Being that all Dimensions are present in any one Dimension, we are everywhere now; moreover, even outside of this bad dream we call reality to sanity with our source - God. We still hold to the group soul's politics of who we are in a group form and what we want to get out of this venture to the highest experiences possible. The First Dimension is very political in ways hard to describe. We plan how we wish to be as Jivas - one to incarnates, for experience and growth in ways different from others First Dimensional realities. So, one seems to establish their basic plan or politic in one's uniquely chosen physical Dimensions of a set of one to eight with finishing Dimensions of the ninth to twelfth. We all have the same basic idea with our politics of growth and experience requested in coming here. That idea is, of our unique set of one to eight Dimensions is, if I may state it again: To - be God - as much as possible. You might study UFO-ology and research into it far in more advanced races than ours and discover that we all have the same underlining agenda of life – to be God.

So, how is it to experience a group consciousness without a separate ego that we obtain in the Second Dimension? The answer is simple – you are still there, but you don't realize it! All Thirty-three Dimensions coexist simultaneously beneath our awareness. Our attraction to each other makes all life possible due to our chosen agenda – to be God' This is the attraction principle. We experience a sense of oneness from the First Dimension in the Wholeness of who we believe God is primarily in one word - trying to be God. Remember, as mentioned in the Hua Hu Ching – any words depicting God are false. The representing of God in a name form explains the factitiousness in such an endeavor to choose a uniquely designed – so-called – oneness that we have chosen and identify as our First Dimension decidedly to be of a false foundation to start. The First Dimension is, to coin a phrase, a one work statement of what you feel God and life are all about; and our needs and intentions to live separately apart from your source to depict it in trying to be God.

We were and are still currently a part of God's Body. In explaining this fact, we must consider that all numbers start with zero, which entails all other numbers are of an imperfect design and nothing

God would have thought of as its outside of God's logic. So, if we had entered the First Dimension, we are still in the positive zero states as sons of God as well. And for that fact, we may be holding to the First Dimension even though we are humans in the yellow zone of the Third Dimension, also. That is why we should view each other as all being family to each other. We similarly view God. In our Dimension, we seem to require a special love from God in the form of wealth, beauty, and the need to be admired by the populous in the misguided attempts of our manifestations of being God Himself.

The self-help new age book: *A Course in Miracles* preaches that we never left God at all, but we fell into a dream corrected in an immeasurably minute slit second or time that we fell in that dream. Since I stated that time was in use, what we call an uncountable number of years is just this split second between God and us. All-time is in the moment of unrealized timelessness. We have the invention of time to analyze just how this insanity can have happened in our Third Dimensional use to time by our use in many incarnated lives. We all can transform in a flicker of the eye back to the Divine if we stop analyzing this insanity that we are in and - *BE*. The undertaken is more so an undoing of the self than an education process which puts all spiritual studies at a disadvantage to Eastern meditations of the void.

In the First Dimension of this falsely called oneness, we had no individual ego but a group soul – Ego. WE – of our larger soul group cut off from the divine from being a drop of water in the ocean that became the ocean itself to a state finite group order of life. Our group soul is a hologram that can be broken down into its most minute pieces and still represent the whole – a semi-sense of oneness but finite simultaneously. The fact of it is genuinely here, even in our Dimension. The essence of it is from the First Dimension that resonates with all others as us being of a group soul or family. We reflect our universe as in our very eyes are all things in this universe that we decided to be a part. In India, a Hindu would greet us as if we were to meet God

Himself. By this very fact, we accredit our inner reality of God as to be God Himself.

In ancient Israel, the holy name is God was announced by using the "Yoh He Vav He" once a year by the high priest of Levi. In the Jewish tradition, the right pronunciation and singing of the divine name would bless all of Israel for one year. The divine name is Neolithic; it represents fire, air, water, and Earth, common with almost every natural religion. We have come to know this faith currently as Wicca. What is an odd fact about Judaism is that it is quite Wiccan in its foundation? They even worship ten angels as gods as likened to Wicca in the Jewish mystical study of the Qabalah. The point being, the First Dimension sounds out our personal name of what and how we feel God regards us. The name of God as we know it is from the Norse language for the word *Goden - invoker*. The Eastern faiths have no representation of their God. The Hindu faith has many names for God, but in Juana yoga, God is you. For that fact, in BuddHism, it is yourself, as well; this is a mission of self-discovery of which we will find that name one day and seeking it apart from the falsities it holds?

The First Dimensions location and substance is of a dot that is everywhere, but not particularly in any location; it is in view in its entirety in any given location. It has no reservation to anyone location alone, in that all references depict are all equal and the same – a hologram. At such a point, are the very roots of our existence in one of the Thirty-third Dimensions? The very tip of a pin is equal to the tip of your nose and can house all its souls equally and the same. You now can say that about any point you choose. We are all there in every dot at any desired location indicate; its location is relative to the cursor, but it's all the same dot. We are all there in that minute dot in a group soul form. I have heard in Theosophy that the kingdom of God is not impossible to view its grandeur, but unthinkable small and microscopically impossible to see.

The OM, as the name of God, may be chanted as Yahweh if you are of the Jewish faith. To learn the divine name of God is essential in our journey back to our source. I can joke about it, saying that it is fictitious and only valid if we are subjected to its hold, as we are currently. The truth is – you are! However, if we can choose another name of God beyond any such name here on Earth or any other planet in our Universe, try it – it may work better.

One question remains: if we knew from the on start that all these names of God are false, why did we try them just the same? Answer: To try to understand the unknowable can only foster insanity as it's impossible. So, insanity is our standard logic, and just the same, God's logic is seen as insanity anyway to us – so what is the difference regardless of to be insane and try the impossible? Trying to understand God can foster insanity, I state final.

In conclusion to this chapter, I am writing – to *follow our bless.* Bliss blesses the self and others equally. Who knows where it can take you? True life is eternity; you have no vulnerabilities; death is a shift to another state of being. Our true creations are with God and outside any numbers used in math and outside any set of One to Twelve Dimensions based on using such math. No human brain can perceive our true creation with God. I can only omit that it does not use math in our set of One to Twelve Dimensions that we created. Yes, what we created is not Divine and is not accredited to God's design. *In healing, that statement,* take a breath and repeat after me – *Be stillness and know we are at one with God.* – Edgar Cayce.

Chapter 8

The Second Dimension Flatlanders

The book *Flatland - A Romance of many Dimensions* by Edwin Abbott was published in 1884 by Seeley & Company of London. The satirical book depicting the pseudonym of "A Square" used the fictional Second Dimensional Realm of Flatland to comment on the hierarchy of Victorian culture; consequently, the book's more enduring contribution is its examination of altered Dimensions. This dated book by Edwin Abbott created the first-ever mention of a Second Dimension to the public. The only statement before Edwin Abbott was by a Greek philosopher Democritus (460 - 370 B.C.E) from Abdera, Greece. Democritus was a rationalist, like Leucippus, another pre - Socrates Greek philosopher. Democritus wrote about alternative universes in higher orders in structure. Only Hugh Everett, in 1957, declared in a lecture that there are alternative universes of higher order to explore.

From here onward, my writings are intuitive and a genius of automatic writing: The Second Dimension is the foundation and planning tablet to all other twelve Dimensions. The mathematicians in the second who planned the grand scheme of life and growth are of the highest order of living souls incarnated in this Second-Dimension Realm to construct life using an extremely high order of math unknown to us. A probable and imaginary mathematical formula, equation generates all matter, energy, and life in our infinite multiverse. This formula is worked in a simple dot that holds all the math needed for its manifestations. This Dot needs to be activated by only two of its Second-Dimension entities to generate its effects and confirmed by a circle of eight others to regulate it to its unique perfections to manifest its realities.

The Minds of the Flatlanders are of the highest order that one can ever imagine. They never planned out their edifices with two pointed straight or curved lines, as we do. As stated, – it was all in the Dot. The plans generated from the Dot are realized in the Flatlander's group's Mind and are made manifest first - *in their Minds,* and second – *in structured for in their worlds.* Essentially, being of a lower Dimension, such overly simple and practical creators are essential to the Dot. The fact is, they used their advanced math most practically. Their Minds are uncluttered by complexities and can think in a focused manner. They have individuality but are functioning in a group manner of joining Minds. Their thinking attempts are aimed at the absolute and not aimed at the finite. We cannot achieve such use of Mind now because we lack higher intuitive training, and the Minds join. I have heard that very advanced alien life forms can do just this now; we need to catch up with them in due time. Get all confused lines and numbers out of our Minds – it's all in the blind faith in the Dot; intuitive access would be needed, though.

Yin/Yang, Heaven/Hell, God/Sons, Good/Bad, Growth/ stagnation - vectors are up/down and forward/back–no left/right – it is the densest of them all. The motto of this dualistic Second Dimension is: In pains, I find joys; in sadness, I find encouragement; In you, I in me; In emptiness, I find wholeness; In neglect, I find love; In poverty, I find riches; In the darkness, I find the light; and in nothing I find everything.

The Thirteenth to Thirty-Three Demi-gods is engaged with those Second Dimension Mathematician to manage the lower twelve Dimensions and allow a failure in the whole system to result in early return to God's sanity. It is interesting enough to know that God planted a worm in our design for us to give up and to return to the

Divine. They use the Dot to work out the math to create the framework for all creations from their Dimension to all higher Dimensions with such a lovable worm of God. God's logic to this is: if flawed logic is used, proper logic corrects. The worms are the purest logic God in our math used.

We, too, can use the Dot to free our Minds for higher reasons, but we need higher intuitive training to manage its applications. As in a single dot, there is no room for interpretation of what we see. Words and images are only of the lower Mind and subject to private interpretation, bias, previous understanding, and personal background. The human brain is Eight Dimensional and can go far beyond our Third-Dimension sophisticated insights. Setting our Minds free and being open to understanding beyond our present scope is the right Mindset. Books of knowledge that we may read are only driving us in the wrong direction. They are all subjective to the author's understandings of the matter. Even this very book we are reading is just one man's intuitive view of matters.

Thomas Merton, a Catholic Priest, and religious scholar, wrote about the misuse of the Mind. He stated that understanding life, God, people, and events are all wrong by trying to find meaning to these things using the Mind. He further wrote that we should not try to understand any of these matters but give it over to mystery with an empathic awareness of what is right that will magically come to our Minds; this is the best use of the Mind, to my knowledge. Merton writes that the truth is beyond the Mind; our vascular responses read truth – keep our ego-based Mind out of it. Why that person does not like you is no concern of yours, but to understand that they do so and let them work it out apart from you. Let them try to understand why they feel that way toward you on their own. Things happen for a reason. Just let them be. I do not believe in saying *I am sorry* and trying to work things out with others. Words seem to get in the way–let things go. I also do not believe in talking things out.

People have a way of uniting on a different forum in time, or they never do. - Such is life. To need a particular person or thing is codependency. I now comment once more about negotiations; it's all done with no words, only empathically getting in the way. Feel the resolution; do not resolve.

Be friends with yourself. Neediness only brings misery and seeking outside of the self. If they are, indeed, our friends, they will return, or maybe it is for the better. Give it over to mystery and have faith in knowing it's all for the best to be alone. I remember a friend who slept it off when he had many problems, and they all seemed to resolve on their own. Subconsciously, he knows God loves Him, and God's Holy Spirit will put all matters right. He also runs away from problems. Running is no solution. If you run, we cannot use the wisdom of the heart.

In a New Ager self-help book - A *Course in Miracle,* the Holy Spirit is our sense memory of our divinity with God and used to create our realities. I wrote God is negative 0, and God's infinite Sons–are positive 0 of one body and inseparable. Even if we miscreate apart from God. He is working to correct it for our happiness out of His Divine love as His regal nature. Yes, those Second Dimensional creatures made use of such with their access of their Minds to the Divine higher lords =/demi-gods *demiurges* "creative spirits" employing their math to create all life.

To describe the environment of such odd Dimensional creatures and the worlds they inhabit. They are missing one vector point. They have up and down, but not side to side as they are flat. There are only three music notes and three-color uses. You cannot sidestep another Flatlander there. It would help if you went around them in other directions to get by them but not to go under them or over them as they do not have the freedom to do so.

They have flat zones to live in, much like planets as we do. They have internal energy sources and are subject to individual evolution to empower them in their personal growth. There are no Suns or Planets there, but zones of self-generated forces. Their light and energy are indeed coming from within, as they should be just the same. We should take a lesson from them.

In one way, they are far more advanced than us; but in another way, higher Dimensional life is more developed than them. All true advancement is a question of us dis-engaging from our First Dimensional Minds. Now we must stop trying to work it all out, which would cause our return to the Divine. We must dismiss any false ideas of God we originally had.

The higher Dimensions of the twenty's demiurges are the actual designer of all things co-working with the groundings of the Second Dimensional creators. In the beginning, all aspects of life's creations calculate mathematically with the Second Dimensions guided with the Demi-gods of the teens and twenties Dimensions. The Second Dimensional lord joins their Mind with the *higher lords* of the most increased Dimensions in a group of intuitive action to make all manifest. All the creation happened in timelessness and opened in timelessness.

These Demiurges of higher demiurge lords are of the Twenty-First to the Twenty-Ninth Dimensions. The twenties are needed as they are open to group involvements which open them up to the divine plan. Such a plan does not have God's approval, not of His origin as sound to Him. Yes, God permitted us to go astray, and He does help us create that He would have never made, out of love for us and an unknowable sense of humor He has. God thus blessed the demiurges of the Twenty-First to the Twenty-Ninth Dimensions with the logic needed to suit our intention in our depiction of Himself - God. God plays along with the crazy idea we have of Him by yielding to our needs to depict Him out of a playfulness He has toward His sons.

As God is the highest, the Tao Te Ching is the lowest; this is God's way of being all mighty. God allows all works of His sons and judges them all not. God is not subject to this miscreation as to have not one an opinion. If we create wrongly, God hears our joys and cries as the same voice, without being affected by any of it. When we call God's help - His Holy Spirit - it is just what we expect God to do and be for us. God is impartial to what goes on in our reality. A helpful God that answers our prayer is a delusion we have of God to respond to our needs here. God helped the demiurges create all our Dimensions of uncountable universes but planned a worm for it to fail. What goes on here cannot be altered by God, as He was not the author. To God's eye, He sees us in His grace and divinity by His side. I am sorry to say; it is your delusion that God answers our prayer. What answers our prayers is your self-love and high self-esteem. If we feel we desire it- it is ours.

I had terrible associates in the past and tolerated them out of disrespect for myself. I respect myself now and do grant myself kinder friends. Though I can be unkind, and I make mistakes. Either way: good deeds reap good karma and bad, bad karma.; and self-respect and self-love always yield good karma. I state now –we are the God that answers our prayer here; even bad people grant themselves their wishes. God does not intervene here. What we call good or bad is relative to our feelings.

This idea of good and evil is a second-Dimensional concept. In our evolution, we shall derive the third concept of indifference to the two; this is one of our growth goals in the Third Dimension. There will be no self-love or self-hate. What will be in the state of non-attached simple beings? We will not need to strive after anything or anyone or to do anything but be. This state will be in a higher Realm of the Third Dimension, though. We cannot achieve it here in our Yellow Realm of the Mind. Yes, in the Second Dimension, they have a sinful Realm and a perfect Realm. Avicii is located there. Avicii is the lowest zone in all creations; the worst souls are sent there to punish evil deeds all over creation.

In the Second Dimension, the godly, highly advanced lords maintain the math used to keep creation going. However, some evil lords propitiate all evil in the Second and Third in our Dimension. The most notorious evil creature there is what we may call the Egyptian god Set. Set, Oden, etc., is both a good and bad God. Many pagan faiths have a good and evil God. This creature handles all growth challenges by helping all to meet their growth challenge. The *Sonography*–Chinese writings - for *trouble* is the same for *growth* in China. The logic is sound, but due to us gaining our self-consciousness, we entered atheistic reality. With no God-reality, we felt that God would punish us in kind.

Our fears of an attaching God convoluted the sound logic of the devil. All evil is misunderstood fear from a non-existing punishing God; this is all subconsciousness for us but emerges in our man-made religion's punishing God with sins and proper behavior to avoid punishment. The devil as we know Him is the negative reactionary aspect of this enlightened principle of growth. The devil will attack us until we have learned self-love. Self-love is the right behavior that usually fosters respect for others and peace. If you have that, the devil can rarely hurt us.

This devil lives in the negative Realm of the Second Dimension. I say now that what is negative is not always bad but the passive attracting principle. This devil's influence is in the Second and Third Dimensions but rarely in the Fourth. The devils' intentions are for us to address our punishing God and laugh at Him. He does have His duties with us, too, along with tormenting us until we had the last laugh. Until then, he is against us. I tried to laugh at the devil, but it only made His torment worst.

The humor needed is God's humor. That is – take nothing seriously; the goal is not the destination but the path itself. Evolution is the opposite of the truth. Just realize that there I nothing of any value here or anywhere. All we need to Be is Be! The homeless ones are indeed God's people. No one takes care of them, but they are provided for anyway. Having means nothing being is everything. You make manifest what you are inside as being!

Most of my unpleasant experiences were out of my inappropriate behavior and bad choices made. I encouraged them on out of disrespect to myself and others. The challenge was to choose for my best interest only. Such demonic forces will set the stage for us to choose right or be punished. Such a devil is our servant and not so bad after all.

Returning now to the Second Dimension, meaning the creators of the second. The Second Dimensional creatures have a wild sense of humor and charm to them. They are witty and clever; they are one for the surprise of others; they love to tell their smart jokes to their friends' amusements; they love to tell incredible stories to entertain their friends. They are considered, by our standard, to be immature and overly simplified in their thinking, though. Engaging in witty conversation is their most famous pastime; they enjoy playing jokes on each other – both good and bad. They enjoy telling – who did its tales, mysteries tales, clever puzzling tales to find it means, and just about anything to expand their Minds.

They are inadvertently attempting the individual cerebral awakening process to gain a unique and special rationale eventually; their brains work along a matrix of inner circles with intersections in a curiously designed pattern. Thoughts emit through an Orange Realm of spiritual energy, but it's more gold than orange. The other two colors are Yellow and Red. Their Red Realm is passive with some evil and violence involved, but they are meant to live life at its fullest like the Red Realm in our Dimension – Arda.

Their Yellow Realm is not yellow, but its energy is mental and joyous. The use of Mind is very different from ours; they get the answer first then ask for the question after; their ways of thinking are seen as counter-intuitive by our standards, though not knowing is not the problem but the being open to too much is. In our use of Mind, we do not know, so we can know.

Our higher level of growth opens an advantage with us in that he knows what we do not know as to them not knowing what they do not know; this makes our Minds mysterious to them. They try it at mystery stories to open their Minds to mystery, but that only gains a shallowest reach of Mind and can't grasp mysteries or mystery in general. Still, their elite can use the dot in a group of higher concepts but cannot see their applications. They are used as a shallow conduit or information to be grounded. They can receive intuitively but cannot sense its applications. Their grounding of the highest mathematical algorithm of life is essential, though with a Second-Dimensional Mind faster than most Universal supercomputers.

Thought any applications to manifestation are beyond them totally. They do not have a higher Mind but can reflect it perfectly in a grounding if needed. We have higher Minds in the Third and is heightened in our Yellow Realm of Mind we are in currently. We seem to know what we don't know which is the beginning to wisdom. We are wise in our Realm we are in. We are meant to gain the wisdom of all ages here on our planet Earth one day. To know the mysteries of what we do not know is our advantage here.

Their Minds are still of a group nature, though. They do everything in groups; they even think in groups and families. Their immature simple Minds allow them not to filter their opinions regarding Universal knowledge to assist them in their thinking, groundings, and creations. They say in our Dimension that it is incredible what children have to say; they even can recall their past lives – our children.

The Second Dimensional souls live in larger circles of even larger ones still - and larger yet. They live in rings or rings or colonies of souls. These circles are in trees of trees. These trees all stem from a central circular tree; in our Dimension, we have, in like manner, planets and galaxies and the Universe. In the Second, they have trees of trees of trees.

As they are two-Dimensional by nature, the total living area of the Second-Dimensional creatures is on one plane. They have zones of higher energies from which they assemble. They do have what we call—campfire entertainments around higher energy spots. The energy spots give them joy and laughter, encouraging them to tell their witty stories to the group. What we call planets in our Third Dimension are large energy zones for inhabitants in their Dimensional reality. Yes, they have clusters of them as in galaxies that we can relate to. What they have for a Sun is just a central point of energy of which only the most advanced souls can be around it. The prime areas of energy we may call planets to revolve around such large primal energy points. In their home life, the souls give energy to their structures. If they leave their house, the house disappears and reappears when they return.

If we were to enter their reality, they would see a point growing into a two-Dimension shape larger and more prominent then smaller and smaller until it is a point again. The souls would witness us as an unexplainable phenomenon that might destroy their structures and them if in the path of us. They would see us in two-Dimension slivers passing by in its destructive way. We would scare the life out of them; and, giving them stories to tell for some time.

You are probably wondering just how much souls look like. They look like a circle with eight legs with four heads at right angles to each other, like half circles protruding from them with a smaller half-circle mark in the top that houses their brains. One brain for each head of four. They have two passive brains and two active brains. The thoughts that manifest projected to the gold Realm affect their worlds. There is a central dot in them that picks up and emits exterior energies via their four brains. This central body dot receiver doubles as a singularity brain to try to explain ideas into straightforward explanations. They try to understand who did it and other tales with that central body dot receiver.

How they travel is interesting, the souls there project outward a line to indicate where they are going, so no others may cross them. They need not eat food as we do but absorb needed energies from their environment from that central energy brain points from the outside in. The inhabitance multiplies by asexual reproduction but chooses to be impressed by *admiring others* to influence the production. Their daily thinking is easy; they create a dot that allows all knowledge to reflect their Minds to its outward manifestation with no personal interpretations.

The Second Dimension was theoretical at first but made physical as soul accepted their intention in such an evolutionary process of depicting God as they see fit. It is a projection of the First Dimensions group, one soul's operation, to attempt the application of our God name in all realities – know God by being Him and our larger depiction of how we individual see God as for each soul. The Pro - Second Dimensional souls and the etheric form of Demi-gods co-creates with the twentieth Dimensional high demiurges of all the Dimensions of the twenties. The Dimensions from thirteen to thirty-three are mostly of Godlike logic, shading with some insane reason used in the lower Dimensions.

Regarding time, they only have the past and future; there is no present time in their Dimension. Our Minds can't conceive of such a concept of time. It is a question of living for what we had in the past; or living the item we will be - the future. I cannot explain it any further than that. There is no present time as we know it there; we are either – past or future. If one chooses to have – they are *physical* and live in what we call the past; if, to be, they are energetic, or angel-like and live in a theoretical state – *nonphysical.* They are yet of a group ego form with little individuality, though. What they like and do not like eludes them all apart from stories. I mean personal likes and dislikes in terms of emotional, heartfelt desires. They have little understanding of who they are; such personal desires and wishes are beyond them out of a lack of self. They are groups souls still like in the first Dimension; they lack self for begin.

Hindu Sages say that anything physical is in the past. The fact is our very existence is the past. In our third-Dimensional time concept, we are trying to understand with our uses of the present what we want out of all of this in *personal recognition of self* to depict God as we see Him. In the Second Dimension, they have not gotten that far yet. They are still trying to understand the God/ Son relationship, as I mentioned above.

In the Thirty-Third Dimension, we can be at one with God and feel His reactions to such a wrong depiction of Him and realize that He loves our depictions of Him and does laugh over it and invite even more of them. We see now that God is narcissistic by nature and encourages His sons to depict Him to time and eternity to His amusement and laugher. The sense of humor of God is beyond all to understand and ever so willing and humble to be seen wrongly, as you can see in those Second Dimensional funny creatures.

Chapter 9

The Third Dimension

Our Third Dimension has three physical realms, with one semi-physical Realm: and three delusive energetic Realms. In recognition of both, the New Agers and Metaphysicians call the delusive energetic realms - the Astral Planes. The first four physical planes of the red, yellow, blue, and Purple are very physical; though, the violet realm is semi-physical in a solid gaseous texture. We live on the Yellow Realm of the Mind; the Red Realm, Arda, is lower to us of quality and vitality. The Blue Realm, our next higher, is the perfect Realm of godly peace and wellbeing. The Purple Realm is semi-physical and semi-energetic but not delusive; it's what we can relate to as heaven. Our transitory plane – our Astral Plane, is used for our regroupings and planning for future incarnations to any Four Realms or beyond.

One thing that sets us apart from most Dimensions is our mult-personality treat of having ever so many unique incarnations. In most Dimensions one returns back to the physical more the less with the same Mind and personality and not uniquely diverse at all. We do this here to analyze our two riddles we all have to resolve. They are: *To be God in the flash and to have a special love from God* – are they all possible? We do this in a subconscious manner and in our dream and fantasies we all have. Yes, odd as it may sound, our crazy fantasies are one of the few keys to unlock the two riddles of life; it's in the failure of them that is our release and peace that is not appreciated or understood at all by us humans.

Before we go on, I shall elaborate on what is a Realm. A Realm is a subdivision in a Dimension. The state of its atoms behaves uniquely to each Realm, causing the like Atoms – Realm Atoms to not co-exist the other unlike Atoms; this causes unlike conducting Atoms to be invisible to unlike Atoms. They all co-exist in the same Dimension but are hidden and unaffected by each other. We call dark energy our universal expansions in the void of nothingness. Dark matter is the paired atom of dark matter to dark energy, manifesting our physical Universe with light energy and matter. Each Realm has these four forces at work as we have and cooperate in ways unique to the Realm in question. Dark energy is the success of our expanding Universe with the dark matter that speeds up our progress and feeds our souls. Both light energy and light-matter help us focus on our Dharma and help us answer the riddles of life conjoin with the other two. Else all growth would be impossible.

What is so particular and essential about our Third Dimension in terms of personal growth? We have chosen to migrate through its many levels to gain a separate ego apart from others to represent what we think of as God by being that God ego in the flesh ourselves; this is the basis of all fame and fortune: Movie stars, singers, musicians, artists, architects, scientists, philosophers, athletes, politicians, authors, etc., are all our attempts to manifest God as we see him. We are also here to be seen and be recognized - even if in a superficial manner. Yes, it is justified for us to walk around in a shopping mall to be seen wearing fabulous clothes and a big hairdo.

The number three is influencing these Realms. The number three, in numerology, indicates creative self-expression that would require witnesses and be appreciated for one's talents. The three talents are especially adept in visual and auditory artistic expression to cultivate and achieve this Dimension. The number three is also: Mind, Body, and Soul; past, present, and future. Nature's energies have their ways to flow in a pattern of threes like ocean waves. Have you ever noted that ocean waves group up in threes and then a pause?

What is meant by the balance of Mind, Body, and Soul: we consciously know and are experiencing what we have come to be in this incarnation. So, we came to be an all-star to have as our Dharma? First, what is Dharma? One's Dharma is the balance of the three to manifest as a reputation in this world. Dharma is the duties we came to this planet to do for others and ourselves. Dharma is not karma. Karma is the law of cause and effect. Many naïve people believe that all karma is terrible due to their lack of education; however, there is good karma too; karma is simply an energy flow.

The ability to live in the present is a gift to instill our Third Dimension. Since the present is ephemeral by nature, the question arises: What is the present -now? Stephen Hawking explains time to be two horizontal lines apart with a vertical line crossing them both. The eternal now and eternal space is the same in our Dimension. Quantum time is an abstract concept to explain. Both the Buddhist and Hindi sages celebrate this eternal now with great joy. They care not for the future and hold no regrets or hurts from the past. They relish in the eternal now! In our Blue Real of our Third Dimension, we will live this eternal now daily, as any needs for food, clothes, and housing, and money and love are all provided there without asking for it. They seem to live eternal lives until they end their lives themselves. Our Purple Realm inhabitances have an understandable concept of time as eternal. The Now is fully understood there like no other Realm in our Dimension. They do have their issues too. They are called stupid and ineffective from time to time, and groups change for a better group in managing the lower Realms.

Our Third Dimension's Spiritual Realm, the Purple Realm is where most religions depictions of where angels reside who serves us. The New Ager calls those decedents of that semi-solid Realm to be our spirit Guides who are helpful agents in service to many of our needs. They help us to be all that we can be and encourage us when times are looking dark? Their bodies and environment are both as three-dimensional as we are, but with inter- realm abilities both physically and mentally influential to us on the Earth. Their Realm resembles an Astral but is not delusive by its nature. Their Realm is non-transformable to the Minds of its inhabitants, unlike our Green Astral. Both the men in black and the moth people are from that spiritually gaseous Purple Realm.

The protective angels who guard our children's sleeping at night are projections are of our Minds; in other words, those Angels are human-made and exist in a delusive realm of our near Astral in their serves to mother's children. One question might be: Do we go there after we die? The answer is - it is between us and our thought adjuster's arrangements with our Ninth dimensional Lords – our Master Spirit. The New Ager calls such a thought adjuster our higher self. With the help of the higher guides, we can go anywhere or even to the absolute divine.

The Purple Realm is awfully close and near to the Hindu's Fourth-dimensional – Heaven. The effect of being with such closeness to the Fourth Dimension has upon that Purple-hued Realm gives it an overwhelming influence of compassion and a loving understanding of others. This power opens them up to service to all lower Realm's inhabitants to aid in their needy prayers.

A Cherub and Seraphim differ a lot from each other. The Cherub brings our prayer requests to our Sixth-dimensional over-soul; a Seraphine brings our prayer requests to your ninth-dimensional spirit – higher self/Master Spirit. These angelic servants have an inter-dimensional awareness. They can help us with an understanding that seems like multi-tasking to us. They are of a non– ego type entity, so expansions of consciousness are easy for them. Egos are pretty limiting. Only in the Fifth Dimension do we start to break free from our limiting ego-self. Cherub "karābu" to bless" is seen in ancient Middle Eastern art as a lion or bull with eagles' wings and a human face; and, regarded in traditional Christian angelology, as an angel of the second highest order of the nine old celestial hierarchies. Seraphin - burning one, are angels seen to be burning because they are of pure spirit. The help from the Seraphin is only for life changes situations and not personal wishes as to the Cherub's service. The New Agers teach that our Masters advisors are of this order of angels – Seraphim's. Spirit guards may be called Cherubs; for that fact, the family member who passed on to the Green Realm may guide us earthbound souls as a spirit guide as well for us.

There are four other orders of Angel in the Catholic Faith: Thrones, Dominions, Virtues, and Powers.

Thrones: Thrones are the Angels of pure Humility, Peace, and Submission. They reside in the area of the cosmos where material form begins to take shape. The lower Choir of Angels needs the Thrones to access God. That high Realm is the Tenth Dimension where all are manifest. The kabala high angel names Metatron is a throne deity. He is the voice of God and gave Moses the Ten Commandments on top of Mount Sinai. Their main duty is to uphold universal. The Egyptian Goddess Sekhmet is also s throne. They can be quite intrusive in doing so which is outside of most angel's standard if lawlessness is kept unchecked, though. They find it a full-time job to keep the balance of the forces in check in Arda.

Dominions: Dominions are Angels of Leadership. They regulate the duties of the angels, making known the plans of the higher forces. They are seventh-dimensional governors who plan new planets with new races to help us all along in our progress. Our planetary donation to all in our Galaxy is an alternative to living in gigantic mother ship space colonies. We are starting to see this in our movies and TV shows.

Virtues: Virtues are known as the Spirits of Motion and control the elements. They are sometimes referring to "the shining ones." They govern all nature; they have control over seasons, stars, moon; even the Sun is subject to their command; they are also in charge of miracles and provide courage, grace, and bravery; and they oversee those in magical faiths like Wicca and rule over to faerie folks in myths. They helped esoteric Christians to obtain miracles in their lives. They are very influential in Arda/Agartha, but far less in our Realm as we need to rely on our intellects and education over the old use of magic currently. I am very magical and use my magic for my success. It's just love that is a hard one for me. They bless our Astrology to make it a tool of personal development and evolutionary changes.

The Powers: Powers are Warrior Angels against evil defending the cosmos and humans. They are known as potentates. They fight against evil spirits who attempt to wreak human beings into chaos. They blessed the United The states of America fought the Nazis and ended the Holocaust and found a curse for small pocks in Europe. They will end the senseless Muslim fighting in due time as well. They kept the wars in Arda to a reasonable level by re-enforcing the good agents there. Unlike the Throne who are must higher, the Powers are more hands on with others and dedicated to their peace and growth.

I have explained the Purple Realm quite well; I will start with the red zone to the blue with its associated energetic realms or zones. But, before I go into the Red Realm, I delineate what exactly a Realm is. A Realm is a subdivision of Dimension. In our Third Dimension, we have three primary realms – Red, yellow, and blue with one semi-physical violet realm, all of which are stagnating. We have three dynamic and energetic realms that are delusive by nature. The total is seven as in our rainbow and our scheme. What is a Realm? It's what one can see and bear witness to our physical Universe that we see and live. Our physical Universe divides into two-part: Three dynamic - energetic and four stagnate - materials. We are currently in a stagnate material universe in its yellow Mind band of manifestation.

The Red Realm – Arda

The Red Realm resembles the three moves: Lord of the ring and Avatar. With the influence of the card game from the nineties – Dungeons and Dragons; with Doctor Who – an old English Television program from 1963 to 1989 BBC productions; and lastly, the book by Ursula le Guinn – The Wizard of Earth Sea. If we have seen both movies and are familiar with the card game and the book, we might have a glimpse into this odd Realm. Our Earth has three other Realms the Red, blue, and Purple. Our Earths is of the yellow Mind/ joy vibration of a Realm but in its respective Realms are interlocked as reflections of each other. Our Earth had an Arda infusion of its violent nature from 1914 to 1945, which caused two World Wars and continued after with the cold war until the Russian changed their government on the 25th of December 1991.

The Red Realm Sun is dim and old. That Sun was the first to manifest, followed by the other four. With a faint Sun, the Planet was dark and cool. The Elohim grew new planets and hybrid trees that gave off a lot of light during the day and ghostly light at night. There are even flesh-eating trees to be watchful of too. The realms vibrate to the red hue making the inhabitance energetic and loving of all things in life. Fighting, drinking, sex, arguing, sports, anger, the passion, and vitality of life are of this hue of that energy. One awakes to the very essence of life itself there. In-kind, if those of the Blue Realm's Earth lose their lust for life, they immediately incarnate to Arda to get it going again and to feel the blood flowing in their veins again.

The advanced race of humans from our Yellow Realm – Elohim, had to immigrate to the Red Realm's Earth – Arda/Agartha, to survive the meteor attacks coming from a young Universe and a cooling planet. Arda's Realms Planet was incredibly cool, so they developed plants to produce carbon dioxide to warm up the environment. Elohim's scientists mistakenly developed plants in our south poles oceans to eat carbon dioxide emitting from volcanoes as their planet was overheating. So, they hybrid plans in the south pole to eat the gas in their original home planet to the yellow Realms Earth – our Realm and Planet that we live on currently. The plants multiplied in a runaway amount resulting in our planet's cooling ever so fast.

Between the meteor's rains and the cooling disasters, they had to immigrate to Arda into the Red Realm. Life was fine for the longest time in our Realm of Earth in their very advanced culture, but the meteor attacks increased beyond their tolerance, with a cooling Earth beyond their tolerance level. They had no other choice but to seek refuge in another level of Earth – Arda. Unfortunately, our Earth Mother Spirit - Gaia, did not like them anyway and made it hard. The reason being is that they did not evolve here on Earth but were from a planet orbiting the star Alcyone. The Elohim did not cooperate with Gaia's four directions in their culture - north-south, east, and west. In our current culture, we have seen in our primitive religions.

There was inhabitance in Arda when the Elohim/Anunnaki arrived. They were animal-like but advanced for their level. So, the Elohim/Anunnaki interbred with the various species and did genetic alterations to hydrate more advanced intellectual species. They even created a less intelligent race called humans in their likeness with genetics from their bodies. Resulting for that world, there are a few species from intelligential to semi-intelligential human-like life to human life as we know us.

The overlords:

Anunnaki – In the Mesopotamian language means – *Those who came from the sky*. Elohim – is a bi-gendered title or helpful angels. The Elohim/Anunnaki are the highest human life form in Arda; they live far apart from the rest of their world in high elevated saucers upon extremely high poles. They are 8 feet tall and blond with light eyes, with two tongues that can speak two languages simultaneously but are mainly telepathic. They use the two tongues mainly for spiritually healing songs for all Arda if asked. The Doctor who BBC television shows depict them wonderfully. They use the five lower life forms as a servant if needed. The Theosophist and New Agers call them the Lemurians. Theosophists also mentioned the *Hyperboreans* too, who I say is from the Blue Realm of Earth.

Forget what the New Agers and Theosophic teaches regarding those three races *Atlantic, Lemuria,* and *Hyperborean,* that they are all from our Realm of Earth is false. - No land sunk under the sea with an advanced Atlantean culture. Fools have tried to look for Atlantis wasting millions of their fortunes on finding it. It is incredible how people can delude themselves.

I studied with the Theosophist in New York City for twelve years, and I feel that they have most of it right, but not all right! To clarify the two races of Elohim/Anunnaki, the Elohim migrated to Arda from our Planet and the Anunnaki seeded from Arda to our Planet. They chose their Human models to be the future race on our Earth. They evolved from the ape's step by step until Cro-Magnon was developed in around 40,000 BCE in South Africa to work the Anunnaki's gold mines. The Elohim/Anunnaki did not interfere with the sub-species but intervened if their wars got out of hand using the Atlantean race. They enjoy their isolation apart from the lower sub-species in Arda.

They are also known as the Anunnaki. The idea that their planet was destroyed was only a change in condition on our very Earth's Red Realm and not a far-off planet. After conditions on Earth were reasonable, they ventured back to use the ape-like inhabitance to mine for gold to help their atmosphere moderate. Over time, they developed humankind as we know it- us. We were gold miners many years ago. Our race multiplying shocked the Anunnaki, and they left us to evolve. They obtain the gold needed, but they help us instill a primitive religion for us as early humans. The Babylonians call their Planet Nibiru, or it can be called Arda. In Babylonian, the name Anunnaki means – *princely blood,* which defines the high-Minded way of the Elohim of Arda/Nibiru?

There are a few species such as:

Humans - they are a downward genetically designed race of blond, blue-eyed people with some darker-haired members with light eyes. They live primitively with some intellect but use magic to aid them as a supplement in their daily lives needs. With the four others mentioned below, the more advanced Human with other advanced species congregates to a stronghold continent of what the New Ager call – The Atlanteans. The Atlanteans use their Earth magic with technology from the Elohim to create wonders. I will write in length in this chapter about the Atlanteans. The Humans Race is the most magic apart from the Atlantean with their use of magical technology. The Humans have the wisdom of the Elohim but in a primitive earthly manner of mysteries, with sorceries, wizards, and magical witches; they like to live in the wet, foggy swampy areas. The other four species find them gorgeous and mysterious and a bit scary, too, with the drama they possess. However, they are the greatest fighter of good and hold one of the Gold Ring of the four white dragons. Therefore, they are one to be favored by the Elohim after the Atlantean colony.

Dwarka – The Dwarkas are half bird-like and half-human and noticeably short and round. They can fly if they keep their weight low and exercise. The older ones are too fat and weak to fly. They are a fighter for good with the humans and fights very well. Their flying abilities help wonderfully in the battle for good. The king of their species is very eagle-like and is known to fight all three evil black dragons with a magical blessing from the humans, with their king wearing one to three gold rings. They do understand Atlantean technology but are not magical at all. They use Atlantean technology and have twenty percent of them who live in the Atlantean community. They like to live part for all others in high mountains and caves.

Fowls – Fowls are tall, half-human, and half of another species that I cannot explain with flat faces. They are the most intelligent under the Elohim and run the Atlantean community. In our culture, we think that human-run Atlantic but No! the Fouls run its culture. They are the second favorite of the Elohim/Anunnaki after the Human race of men. Odd, but only twenty percent are of the Atlantean community. The rest live in tall trees eighty feet high and even feed there too. The tree dweller utmost them make use of advanced technology if needed but ignore it to a simpler life. They seem to have the answers to life's problems for all the species on that Planet. Even the Atlantean and the Elohim ask them for advice due to their intellect. I meant to say that eighty percent of those Fauls who live in the trees have the most brains as the Atlantean Fauls are far too convoluted in details. The best use of the Mind is its simplicity.

Dweeds – Dweeds are primarily human with causation features like the Indian of India but with Angolan black skin mixed with another species unexplainable to describe. They are evil and war-like. They occupy one-third of the Planet. They worship the three black dragons who are against the four good white dragons. They are magical and try to cause chaos, using their magic to please the three evil black dragons. Wars in Arda are non-stop. War is far more often in

Arda than in our realm of Earth. War is an everyday occurrence and like style for Arda. The Dweeds with the dark Mermaid falsely tried to make a peace agreement with the King of Atlantis a foul but gave an amulet that seemed very positive at first. The charm was cursed and cursed the wearer. The king of Atlantis became insane and performed unnatural magic, which condemned the whole Planet. The amulet was taken away and broken in time. One of the evil dragons made the amulet for the Atlantean king's corruption of his soul. It took three hundred years to break that curse. For three hundred years, the wars were the worst ever. The world population dropped by forty percent but recovered by one hundred years after the curse was broken. The curse was broken by the Elohim gift of three gold rights to fight evil. The gift was made fast enough after the curse, but it took a long time to heal from the affliction of the Planet.

Mermaids - Mermaids like Sirens are dark and magical powers in the ocean. They work with the Dweeds. The loving mermaid lives closer to land and in lakes and rivers. The loving one sings healing songs for all and likes to sing at essential weddings and birth. The evil ones are deep ocean black Mermaid who lives in communities deep under the ocean. Both have legs to walk on the land and can breathe air. They need citric anyway and harvest citric often, so both are seen frequently on the ground. They look like blackfish with barely human/fish-like heads. The lovable ones are more human-like with almost human-like faces but not quite totally.

Dragons - There are seven dragons, four good and three bad. These dragons make their predominant in their world; the good leading dragons gave three rings to the three leading young wizards of Arda. One was of the men species- Human, and one to the Foul and Dwark species each. The evil black dragons gave a rod of power to a wizard of the black mermaid and Dweed's species under the ocean to fight the three valent disciples of good. Yes, the Atlantean under the Elohim order can balance the battles if needed.

The Atlantean community

The Atlantean community is a region of Arda influenced by the great and lofty Elohim in their high towered saucers living ever so high and apart from all. They hybrid several species to a higher level to relate to them better, as I wrote. They decided to create a center of advanced inhabitances with a mixture of their natural Earth magic and technology as an experiment. The need for the species evolution was scheduled for them as indicated from higher Realm and Dimensions. The war between good and evil is needed for those souls to decide on personal values and moralities. One would think that the Atlantean's highly advanced technology might stop all the wars. Most truly, they only fight the evil lords if the evil is far too aggressive and dominant. The Atlanteans model themselves after the Elohim and enjoy their lives in their remote sub-continent of Arda. The Atlanteans flying saucers with their laser beams can halt the black dragons but not kill them. Only with the Elohim orders do they intervene in Arda affairs. For the most part, they serve Arda as their doctors and technology salesman. The Atlantean king only had one mistake in caring for their planet. I wrote about it in full a page or two ago.

Theosophists teach that the Atlantean set back their process by a million years, but that is only true for a few hundred years and does not affect our Realm. They did have a dark period of three hundred years of very odd experiments. Atlantean, who can play with life itself of a particular region? A territory of Atlantis was wrongly terminated with its inhabitants of animals, plants, and insect lives due to a cursed amulet given to their king by the Dweeds and dark Mermaids. They maintained the Planet's weather with help from the Elohim. Theosophists teach that the Atlantean changed the climate, but the Elohim did; however, they even say that the Atlantic is no more, but they are still there in that red Realm's version of our Earth.

Conclusion of the Red Realm of Arda:

The Elohim/Anunnaki of our early Earthly Realm immigrated to Arda through a periodic opening and closing of the north's poles inter-dimensional portal. The entry into their Realm transformed their planet into a tropical wonderland of warm and abundant food with hybrids of intellectual to semi-intellectual species of human to half-human species hey hybrid. The only species that we can relate to are the magical human species. They look like their Elohim parents' human race but with the head of our size than the ones of the Elohim / Anunnaki. The Elohim did foster a human race again on our Realm of Earth after the global ice melted; that took millions of years, but we are the result of their works now. The so-called Illuminati members are in Arda as the Elohim, Atlanteans, and others with very secretive advanced Earthly humans incognito.

The other subraces to the Elohim / Anunnaki were quite magical due to the energies of that Realm. The low intellect had them rely on such magic as their higher Minds were not developed yet. Only the elite of the Atlantean had high reasons, and with their technology from the Elohim, they were the primary rulers of that Realm.

The wars between good and evil forces instilled the love of the good over the bad as its appreciation of being good over evil. They needed those not-stop wars to choose sides and identify the good as being good as their nature.

The yellow Realm:

The Yellow is our Realm of the Third Dimensional Earth. The Mind cultivates in this Realm. No longer do we need to rely on our magical abilities like in Arda. We have the use of both our lower Minds and higher Minds like the Elohim/Anunnaki do. The cultivation here is of the Mind and education with needs in using our Mind to achieve outstanding accomplishments like the pyramid of Giza, sending men to the moon, quantum physics, and the following of higher math yet to come.

The Elohim in Hebrew translated – from the sky; and the Anunnaki translated from Babylonian – princely blood and the sky as well; being that they are both the same, our human race's forefathers are – elite human species from the sky. They hybrid us in Southern Africa from the prime ape ages ago over time, step by step until they came up with a human species they can use to mine for gold, as stated earlier. We multiplied in number beyond what the Anunnaki could manage. The bible myth of the Garden of Eden and the forbidden fruit was against the Anunnaki order by harvesting the fruit of a sacred tree that helped the Anunnaki survive in this odd world. They were conditioned to live on Arda and lost their tolerance for our Earth's conditions. They got sick after not eating that fruit. Their allotment of gold has been met anyway, so they left.

All the early humans could leave the camps and explore their planet as the grasses grew to the farthest reaches of our planet. The Neanderthals weren't very useful to our forefathers but highbred to a reasonable level enough to do some work. Still, they needed a higher intellect to do their primary jobs, which leads us to believe that we did technical work too, like information technology and manufacturing aircraft.

We were hunter-gatherers until 40,000 to 50,000 B.C.E. We started to farm wheat, barley, oats, and rice. In the year 3808 B.C.E., at Saqqara, for the first dynasty's King Anedjib built the Step Pyramid was built in 2630 by the Pharaoh Djoser and finished in the fourth Dynasty Egypt – 2567 to 2565 B.C.E. The pharaoh Khufu built the great pyramid of Giza. 2100 B.C.E. The Ziggurat at Ur and the temple were built around 2100 B.C.E. by the king Ur-Nammu of the Third Dynasty of Ur for the moon goddess Nanna, the divine patron of the city-state. Ziggurat "Etemenniguru," meaning temple whose foundation creates an aura. The aura was nothing more than a feeling of a positive vibration of love and peace after the great culture of Egyptian, China, the Roman Empire, us the Middle Ages brought us fabulous, architected buildings.

Many cultures have employed magic, but their main objective was engineering, architecture, law, the arts, and medicine. We still have some magical religions such as the Shino of Japan and Wicca of the U.S.A. and Europe with some African religions. Such magic only serves a minor role in our lives. Japan tried to use their magical Shino priest to create a fortune for Japanese companies in the '80s, but it turned on them after with problems they could not resolve. The Japanese need to support third-world nations financially to lose the curse they have currently. In Arda, Magic was foremost. In our yellow hue of the Mind Realm, it is our Mind solely. Yes, our earlier cultures used magic, but now we need to move away from it totally and work on our Minds exclusively. Education and technology and higher math rule our Realm of the yellow hue.

Education is no longer for the wealthy who can afford it and the upper classes; it is for all men and women to obtain. The internet opens all to the world library of wisdom for all to learn. We will join our alien neighbors in time and live on floating cities above the land and outer space in space colonies. It won't be until we transmigrate into the Blue Realm hue of energy where we will use magic the right way as never before seen in the Red Realm. As for God and religion, we must learn it using education and research what concepts best fit our lives to aid us in our lives. We will come to know that God serves us and not us God.

The Mind rules the Yellow Realm we live in; our Minds are meant to expand here. Magic with some technology for the Atlanteans and Elohim was the norm in Arda/Agartha but not nearly as much in our Yellow-Mind Realm. Yes, there was a very magical culture in our past, are still a few remaining. Japanese priest in the early 80s Japan used their magic to grow the Japanese economy and make sure businesses were rich, though not without consequences. The Japanese economy took many decades to adjust from their bad karma and the disaster of using magic. Any successes they acquired were short-lived. Magic on that level is still possible but inconsistent with our current energies now. We enjoy the faith called Wicca. This faith used old-world magic. However, I feel their magic is of the lower realms and not conducive to soul evolution. I think only superficial growth is possible.

A Swedish singer named Avicii employed a demon to grant him talent in the music world but died according to his contract with the demon of seven years. That is a lower realm's magic. I feel the monster were somewhat evil/good elves of a lower realm than ours. Morality is different in that Realm, as we can see as the elves' magic is amorally excellent and evil. I, too, have worked with elves of the book of Abramelin myself. I've found them to be helpful.

Technology, education, science, and good government are our Yellow Realm of the Mind's keynotes. Our future achievements will seem even more magical than the magic of Arda/Agartha ever was. We will even go beyond in growth in respect to the Elohim of the Red Realm. I state that due to that Realm's disability of accessing the higher domains of the Mind, the Elohim are not using their Minds to the fullest as they did when they lived in their original homes of our Realm. Yes, their technology is far more advanced than ours, but we will outpace them in due time by far. That will be the time when they emerge from their lower Realm to rejoin our world again. They are human-like but with very odd feathers and head and eye sizes. They are ghostly white and tall. They will stand out in a big way when they come to join us. They will be here for their growth as in their old Realm is quite stunted for them.

Time travel in our Realm will be possible. We will need all nourishments from plant life and, unfortunately, will need some from the animal kingdoms. One day in the future, we all will be vegetarian with only synthetic meats grown in laboratory factories for mass consumption. Such meat will be of living tissue but with no consciousness of life. Such cultivated meats will be of the plant kingdom. We will have chicken, beef, pork, and fish. Eggs and milk will be cultivated similarly to today's standards but without hormones with humane animal treatments; there will even be cultured meat unknown by taste or sight by today's public.

In higher Dimensions, one can travel back in their current life to choose again more wisely. Such repetitive regrets in our lives will change our destiny to relieve that old scenario and choose a wiser course of action. Oddly enough, the worst experiences may have mysteriously been the best unrealized to the soul. Most regrets and wanting to choose again might only produce standardized behavior and outcomes that are superficially unproductive to the soul. Our human brains are not that deep always to know what is best. In astrology, degrees of one hundred and fifty indicate these scenarios of life. Most people are far too shallow to see its rewards in such disasters of life when one takes up time travel; it's rare but only done by the advice of many skills advisors to proceed with the adjustment needed.

Arda/Agartha had the same restriction regarding and time travel is hard if not impossible. Though, regarding food in Arda/Agartha, they mostly eat root vegetables as Sun grown vegetables are only night-shads with heady greens. This diet makes its inhabitance mostly short, fair, and stocky. Meats are eaten by the lower classes in the red Realm. The higher life forms there are vegetarians with some greenhouse green leafy vegetable they are hybrids. The sun in the Red Realm below us is far too dim for the green leafy plant. We are lucky in this respect to have these greens.

The blue Realm:

The Blue Realm is our next higher in evolution for us to incarnate to in our Third Dimension. This Realm is still physical like its two lower cousins – the Yellow and Red Realms. Peace is much easily obtained there than on the lower Yellow and Red Realms of our Earth. However, sadness and a general lack of interest in life experiences there. The color vibration of their Earth is blue, so the inhabitants are subject to its wavelength's effects upon them: to the best -Peace, medication, health, spirituality, the stillness of Mind, good sleep, righteous behavior, truth. To the worst: boredom, inertia, passive thinking, lack of ambitions, alcoholism, drugs, depression, failure in life, meaningless in life, suicidal thoughts…etc.

In this Blue Realm of Earth, the world has a peaceful central government. The governmental figures in charge take orders from higher sources beyond their Minds to govern the Planet. I feel Shambhala is a semi-physical Purple Realm is a central governing seat of power. They may even take guidance from the Fourth Dimension as well. The worst effects of their blue wavelength are their main concerns, such as boredom, inertia, depression, lack of life's purpose, and lack of energy. Since there are no wars or poverty, all they can tend to are personal happiness issues.

In this Realm, we have six sexualities: 1- Straight, 2-Homosexual/lesbian with like manner genitals, 3- men with vaginas, 4 females with male genitals, 5- same-sex attracted men with vaginas, and last 6- same-sex attracted females with male genitals. The idea of sexuality was lightly mentioned in The Secret Doctrine by Helena Petrovna Blavatsky in 1880. She wrote about the rounds and the races but has never been delineated to its full until now. Her book also mentions the Purple Realm being gaseous but simply semi-physical and can be from physical to ethereal. It serves its purposes. In our Yellow Realm, we have straight and homosexual/lesbian. However, we show signs of a blue realm shift in our world's growth with transsexual men and women. Such appearance of these transsexuals only shows a progression for us as a race on the world level.

Being that death and disease are not in their world culture, their life spans are unlimited. A computer calculated if the man had an infinite life span, how long might one last. They reported that one could only live seven hundred years until one would die of a fatal accident. In a more advanced Realm, one can imagine that number might be more than doubles to under two thousand years at best. Their inhabitants are youthful until they choose to pass on or die of an accident. From what I know intuitively, only a government official can last that long. Most decided to die out of a lack of life's purpose and a desire to incarnate to a new life. As I said before, sadness and a lack of sense is an issue in that blue Realm.

So, we see that challenge of life there is purpose and ambition. If one continually experiences such challenges, they might tell them that they are not ready to live in such a realm and be further advised to incarnation in the two lower realms of the yellow and red to ignite passions in life. If life passions are not already in the Blue Realm, they will have horrible lives there.

They have a different use of Mind found only in the blue Realm. Such a Mind is open to outer worldly influence for the advantage of the soul there. The bad part raises the question of our soul's separation from our source and a need to reunite again with God; this can make any effort in life futile and meaningless. Many souls return to sanity and rest with God from this Blue Realm of our Planet Earth. The sad one's lacking is the focus and vision that need to be seen as unique and recognized as a godman. The central theme of our Third Dimension of being a specially recognized godman is confused with overly passive spiritual thinking of surrendering to God and to forget it all. A few incarnations to Arda would wake then us a bit.

The question of life's passion in the Third Dimensional and our set of One to Eight Dimensions of knowing God by trying to be Him – or to say, related to our dimension – being a specially recognized Godhead? To do such a task, one must be self-focused to being. The blue hue energies of this Realm expand one to the Divine and a way for the self. A balance between the Divine and the Egocentric is needed in this Realm. Far too often, one is just passive and off-center with the self there. So much is perfect in government, world, money, and relationships that take all of them for granted and flow along in life with minimal purpose or passion. The world's population in character in this Blue hued Realm has a passive nature to it. Finding one's passion, ambition, and purpose for living is required in this paradise world.

In the Blue Realm, they gain sustenance from energy emitting plant-like life forms and fields of grass-like live forms. Landmasses do emit needed energies for life. There are also energy centers large and small throughout their planets to gain required substances. They do not eat food as we do or farm or raise livestock. The animals and Planet are left untouched by the humans living there. Their planets are like a nature reserve, and they live at one with their environment in peace with it like the Native Americans of North America. The elemental life form, such as the elves helping the population in their inter-engagements to create joy or hardships, are needed for their highest growths. The elemental Faery life forms are seen as both good and bad there. They are only bad if one is out of tune with nature as sad or bored or lacing a life purpose. There are even storytelling Elf witches there who brews up chaos for the sorry for their awakenings to a higher source and growth.

Their Minds need to be more self-centered with a goal in Mind; the Mind needs to be less passive as in being a drop in the ocean and to otherwise standout! What their inhabitance is excellent at are their powers and health! They are very strong there and able to do a lot if driven by passion. Many are passionate and lead their worlds in their fame and fortunes gains. I wonder if we can say the same about our Yellow Realm. Possibly, but in our Realm, we are more aware of ourselves than in their trans-personal Realm. They lack self-there to the trans-personal group/world body. We are more independently Minded here in our Yellow Realm. Awareness of our Third Dimensional theme is apparent here than in the blue-hued Realm. All-in-all, trans-personal is achieved there in one's inter-reactions as all is done for the good of all the world. There is not much selfish behavior there. Though, the use of self-centeredness could ignite their passions and a sense of purpose. Then again, I say, it's a balance between the self and the whole.

The Purple Realm of Shambhala:

There are only three genuinely physical realms in our Third Dimension ruled by the primary colors of Red, Yellow, and Blue. This Purple hued Realm is semi-physical but not passive to the Mind as an Astral of the Orange, Green, and Indigo Realms are. The purple is active because its inhabitance uses its environment for real growth compared to a passive environment that gives in the wishes of the Mind and cuts down on growth. The dark energy and matter give – Sweet Atoms to feel them and make them grow. No Astral has access to Sweet Atoms. The Green Realm is the most robust Realm, though. This strength makes it the most popular and most populated with very advanced cultures and Universities of Life. Some might say that the Hogwarts School of Witchcraft and Wizardry had a Green Astral double, or perhaps it was on the Earth's Blue Realm of vibrations. The Earthly School of Hogwarts was in the Scottish Highland in the 10th Century established by the minister of magic in Scotland.

There was high magic school in various parts of Europe in those days as the energies of the Age of Pisces were at their peak then. I cannot say where it was short of saying that in Arda, they had numerous institutes of Real magic. Being that a dragon is mentioned in the book, I might say that Hogwarts had a double in Arda were flying on broomsticks was possible, and inter-reaction with the evil dragons. The motto of Hogwarts is - Do not tickle a sleeping dragon. Only in Arda/Agartha are there dragons, so where do you think Hogwarts was?

The Blue Realm can work spiritual realities in with the physical. Still, one is more influenced by their environment there with the power to cause fundamental changes – in other words – magical Godlike lands to draw divine Energies must as particular Mountains. Lakes, Rivers, and Valleys are all sacred areas to meet God. We call them vortexes here and are loosely chattered all over the Planet. In the Blue Realm Earth, they are far more numerous and much stronger than ours in the yellow Realm Earth. The description of God's country is a majestic landscape, but in the Blue Realm Earth, it's most of the Planet; this makes spirituality more popular. I do not mean religious studies but spirituality which is what values all religions have in common. We have been growing spirituality from the mid-1800s in the USA to the New Aged Alternative Spirituality movement of the 1970s. In 2012 I published a book with Balboa Press called: The Enigma of God, a revelation to man by Frank Marcello Antonetti. I encourage you to read it after this book you are holding now with Esoteric Christianity of the Dark Ages Renaissance times.

The six Kumaras of Shambhala are in charge there under the great Lord – Sanat kumara – Eternal youth and Lord of the twin flames of the kundalini. He is also known as the Lord of all three Earth in its various realms and is a solar ruler. The seven kumaras are: Sanat kumara, Sanatana kumara, Sanandana kumara and Sanat kumara, Sana and Ribhu. The seven all have children's appearances to them. They all travel together and change the different aspects of life in the three Realm and their own. The seven are creative forces that brought in the format of good living to all third-dimensional Realms. Our very own Planet had it near disaster in its earlier days, six hundred million years ago. Sanat Kumar, who resided on the planet Venus, asked our Solar Logi to adjust matters under his management. Sanat Kumara incarnated to our Yellow Realm Earth with the Divine Mother Rukmini as Pradyumna many years ago when Earth hosted our parent race – the Anunnaki/Elohim.

He grounded the magic needed for the adjustments required for the healings of India. Thus, to our Earth, Sanat Kumara was incarnated to do his work. The planetary Logi of Venus Lucifer superimposed his ways of management upon the new Indian population and caused considerable confusion for growth here on our Earth. For a while, the Indian, with many others, almost all died if not for Sanat Kumara of Shambhala's Earth magic ritual he performed in India. The Indo-European tribes such as the Brahmins, Ahirs, Jats, Rajputs, Meenas, Gurjars, Khatris, Tarkhans, Kambojs, Banias, and Dalits establish a culture in Northern India. Sanat Kumara was born as a Brahmin in Northern India. He employed Lord Krishna to stop the wars with the Dravidians of South India, resulting in the story of the Bhagavad Gita with Sanat Kumara's help. His ritual and the books were the healing and the coming of a new Indian Philosophies - Hinduism.

Shambhala is a multi-world government that has a parallel location over the Gobi Desert and the Mongolian border. The blue Realm receives direction directly from Shambhala; our Earth's Realm only receives the evolutionary progress overall from that Realm. The Red Realm of Arda/Agatha has seven dragons who receive guidance. The four good one obeys every work from Sanat Kumara, but the three evil dragons challenge those commands of governing. The Atlanteans and Elohim listen to the four good dragons but see reasons for the three evil ones that foster unbridled passions and will to be needed.

The Third Dimension's Seven Realms
in terms with the Seven Chakras

The Sahasrara Chakra – a thousand peddles in Sanskrit is situated in Shambhala and the whole of the angelic and magical Purple Realm. This chakra gives this Realm head command as the chakra rest on top of the head; there is an indigo realm of a lower vibration to the purple but higher than the blue Realm. The chakra there is the third eye, the Ajni chakra, or in Sanskrit – blessing. This chakra-wheel of energy connects the Mind to the larger Universal Mind under the Hindu god Brahman. The Sanskrit word Brahman translates -the highest Universal principle. The Blue Realms inhabitance uses this Indigo Realm to re-system and plan future lives in the Blue most likely but can be in the lower Yellow, purple, or Red.

This Indigo Realm is an Astral, meaning their environment is passive to their inhabitance Minds. If in trouble, they might go back to our Yellow Realm of cognate awareness or the Red to re-awaken their anger and passion for life again as survival is the key there as it is here too, but not in a dangerous way. Between the Blue and Indigo Realm, one can reunite with their source and father to be of His sanity – many do just that or incarnate to lower Realms for a re-awakening? This Mind/environment relationship can cause self-deluded experience and is the same in the Green and Orange Realms. However, in the Agni center of the Indigo Realm, can be accessed all Universal Knowledge for our highest growths. The understanding of duality is opened there to let us know that both forces of good and evil are there for our highest evolution and to let us understand that all good and evil are an illusion. We learn a more objective way of viewing life is our blessings there in the Indigo Realm.

The blue Realm's chakra is in the throat – the Viśuddha, English: "especially pure" The presiding deity of this chakra is Panchavaktra shiva, with five heads and four arms, and the Shakti is Shaking.

Rightfully so, as in the Blue Realm, we have the purity of soul in its inhabitance. However, they are human with many issues to overcome but still relatively – Pure of soul there. In the Blue Realm, vocal singing is at its most healing. There are some famous singers there who can heal disease just by the singing of their songs. They are also telepathic in the Blue and only use the voice for their healing songs.

The Green Realm is an Astral, as explained before, and it is pretty self-delusive. This chakra makes growth very hard and only allows one to expand on their selves. Education and preparation for future incarnation are done in universities there in the Green Realm. Yes, there are lands with cities for those at rest from incarnations to live a life there. The lower Green seems quite physical, but it is not. The Orange, Green, and Indigo Realms are energetic and passive to the Mind. It may only respond as physical because its inhabitance requires it to be so. Those Realms may appear as a spiritual, ethereal Realm, if need be, to its inhabitance. The chakra in the Green Realm is the Heart chakra – Sanskrit - Anāhata, English: "unstruck" or unaffected – no vulnerabilities or heart chakra is the fourth primary chakra refers to the Vedic concept of unstruck sound (the sound of the celestial Realm). Anahata is associated with balance, calmness, and serenity. Those who pass through this Realm or choose to reside there for an eon gain a heart-centered awareness. Inner growth is possible there stemming from physical incarnations. This Realm serves as our afterlife and is the most populous Realm due to the vitality of the heart chakra. The residents there are influential and live happy lives.

Not all can reach that Realm after death. They dwell in an Earthly reflected state of energy that feels and looks just like Earth, but it shifts its powers because it is affected by our moon. For those lost after that a bad Earthly dead or no spirituality, a police force was needed to gather those lost and march them to the Stone head. The hollowed-out head is covered with silver plating. They enter the head and are set up in individual live support chambers for the long inter-Realm ride.

Upon arrival, they are escorted out of the Stone Head to meet up with their life advisors, who know their hierarchies of guides and Master Spirits. The stone head is needed because the tube of light that most of us used to get to the higher Green Realm is cut back and is out of use due to damages. The trip in the Stone head is long and rough to those who cannot project themselves there with ease. Life support controls their health as inter-realm travel the unnatural way can be dangerous. Who is to say that we have trouble projecting our nature to the other side of life? If this sounds like the 1974 thriller movie Zardoz, you are right; however, the destination sounds more like the Blue Realms perfection of a false paradise lost. The two main stars in that film were Sean Connery and the then young and gorgeous Charlotte Rampling.

Our Yellow Realm chakra is the solar plex. In Sanskrit - Manipura - is a *gem-like city of fire of the Mind.* What it does seem like is a sizeable gem-like temple complex dedicated to the fire of the Mind. Many of our world temples, Universities, and Cathedral are centers of education and were our first used as universities. Columbia University in New York City looks like a gem of a city inside a city, and higher seats of learning are akin to the Yellow Realm. The fire of Mind is ignited to trigger all possibilities of growth; this is the central theme of our Realm – Education and self-awareness. Both Saint Patrick's Cathedral and Saint John the Divine is famous for their design and presentation. I served as an Acolyte in Saint John up on Cathedral Lane for twelve years. Saint Patrick's Cathedral was always a midtown stop to pray in the Aquamarine temple dedicated to the Virgin Mary. Pope John Paul called Saint Patrick's a gemstone in the middle of New York City; and felt so much security in his heart knowing the locales have such a Cathedral. Yes, in Europe, there are so many Cathedrals beyond description, with the Hagia Sophia of Istanbul – The Temple/Cathedral/Mosque of Holy Wisdom.

The Orange Realm chakra is the social Chakra over one's bladder – the Svādhiṣthāna, in English means: "where our being is established.

131

"Swa" means self, and "adhishthana" means established.) This sacral Chakra can boost creativity, manifested desire, and confidence. This Realm is an Astral like the three other ones listed. The Red Realm uses its higher vibrations for their planning of future lives like any other Astral. Though, the inhabitance there is not much more developed than what we find in the Red Realm. There is an aquatic sub-Realm of Mermaid souls. They helped humanity with government and farming knowledge and kept life stock from year 50,000 to year 30,000BCE in Mesopotamia.

We read this in the Mesopotamian culture's very early days, sighting the fish-man who brought civilization from the deep ocean to their world. It was not our planet's deep ocean but the marine areas in the Orange Realm. Apart from marine life, we have the dry sub-realm Fae race of folk that host magical Elves, both good and bad. Both sub-realms serve to keep a root-level type of magic needed in our Third Dimension for all growth. Their Chakra runs all forms of intermingling in the Third Dimension. In the Orange Realm, they are very sexual and success oriented. They try to help humanity in their magic of a one-pointed focus of thought to drive humanity's success forward. Elves of all sorts are willing to help us on our planet to be all that we can be. This Orange Realm has a reflection of our Realm, being that it's right under us. Many Fae folk from the Orange Realm live in an inter-Realm between the two in a large, forested area of our planet, which is the third sub-realm race of Fae folk. Invite the Fae folk into your Creative Visualization practices today – they are all on your side.

The growth of humanity's land use caused hardship on them. They fight back with global health crises like HIV, the small pocks, Covid 19, and the black plaque of Europe. Yes, they can be nasty if provoked. In three hundred years, we lost 1.5 billion hectares of forest. There were 5.5 hectares at one time, which was half of the world's forest coverage. Now we have 4 billion hectares, and 31 percent of the global land in the world is forested. The United Kingdom, apart from its West lands, Galway and the Northumberland's forest, has nearly lost all of its forested lands and wetlands. Most of Eastern Europe lost too much forest to mention. China now is the leader in replanting lost forests. At one time, our deep breathing was eighteen percent deeper compared to now.

I have a house Brownie whose name is "lic lic." He protects me from other hostilities in my house. I also have employed Fae Folk from the book of Abramelin. They demand loyalty and develop a rapport with humans that invokes them; otherwise, they will ignore our requests for help even if our signals are drawn perfectly. They are akin to the Enochian angel though the Enochian souls are between the two Realms of Orange and Indigo: Orange for more personal issues and Indigo for spiritual matters and growth. The Enochian words with a well-drawn out a signal drawing of Angel names to invoke both high and low. The Enochian magic system is more modern, but I felt the Angels/Fae Folk of Abramelin has far more present in our world. If it makes us feel better, the two Fae Folk or Angels classes have helped me out in numerous ways. I care not to write about myself, however. All can email if needed with any questions.

The Red Realms chakra is at the root of us by the anus. Mūlādhāra, in Sanskrit, beams the source of one existence. Survival is essential in the Red Realm due to its violence there. One establishes their physical bodies there and experiences the passion of being in the flesh. However, the Purple Realm encourages many higher developed souls there who Shambhala can arrange and bless. Amongst its many wars, there is peace, love, and joy there too. The very blood of life ignites in the Red Realm of Arda like fighting, sex, anger, personal power, egotist, wars, shallow thinking, etc. For its advantages, it has its disadvantages as well. With help from Shambhala, one's overall success guarantees one's happiness and joy in life.

To conclude on the Third Dimension, I will bring up the study in numerology the number three. If one is good and two is bad, then three is unaffected or indifference to both. To be unaffected by dualities of life protects one from harm but to instill this is beyond most people's abilities. Also, to have an objective view toward life is essential in our Third Dimension. The Buddha raises far above the realms of chaos which is duality. This is our task at hand to accomplish before we can enter into the Fourth Dimension.

The Third Dimension's Realm polarities

- + The 3 solid realms of red, yellow, and blue are negatively charged stagnant and is of an attracting energy of yin.
- + - The three astral realms of, green, orange, and indigo are yang positively charge dynamic and repealing.

The 6 fluid astral are + -

- + Red upper is: +fluid astral hot orange, +-solid astral, the orange realm, + the fluid light orange.

Lower to the yellow though

- +Yellow upper is: + low fluid astral olive, + -solid green astral, + the high fluid turquois astral

Lower to the blue realm

- +Blue upper is: +fluid indigo astral, +- solid astral purple realm, +fluid astral magenta.

Upper and lower to the red real is the same as above.

Astral Realm of + - gay boy like, drama, music, art, culture, learning, sexy,

lower + - +, higher + - + faery like, lower can be trickster,

Solid realm - +

The color frequency is the energy value.

Solid realm – bitch hard mother, bitchy boss, discipline, tradition, rules,

Chapter 10

The Fourth Dimension

This place is the Dimension where we come to know our imagination. Regarding the inner person, we want to project publicly. No one has hidden dreams or fantasies there. All our soul's desires are made evident to our associations and the world in due time. We no longer wish to be known and recognized as a Godman made manifest as in our Third Dimension. However, we are still under our One to Eight set Dimensional theme of knowing *God by trying to be Him*. The Fourth Dimensional soul reveals itself in their imaginations. Their inner dreams are not hidden as one's dreams are renewed from the inner soul in a lifelong cycle of visuals reinventions of the self, like a female pop starlet perpetually reinventing herself.

The cycle is: the inner soul looks like appoint of light from their solar plexus as the outer soul appears as the older soul at large. That point of light will grow and overcome the external soul's body. As the inner soul reaches the halfway point, the external soul decreases in size and eventually shrinks into a point of light in the Fourth Dimensional soul's solar plex. As the point of light shines bright, it grows again to overcome the external soul, body again in an endless loop. This projection is in six cycles of renewal: all four directions with top and bottom.

But is an individual a superficial attention-getter pop star to be adored? No! As self-worship and the need of worship from others are of the previous Dimension – not the fourth! So, why the need for public validations? Well, depth of Mind is exercised there, and one would meet an array of souls – advanced or primitive. At worst, what they are primitives are seeking is empathy is finding like-Minded friends and colleagues. This Dimension is very clique-like and fashionable. Both fashion and design are studied here to focus on one's inner beauty to be project outwardly. Our fourth Dimensional influence on us causes our planet inhabitance to be far more fashion and design-oriented than us not having the fourth influence upon us all. A third-dimensional races rarely have such a polarity to the Fourth. When they do have it religious art, well-designed religious buildings and fashion are seen and is their primal motivating drive for self-development, as with us. When such polarity to the fourth happens in our galaxies and Universes, the races are usually tall with flowing head hair and a human type of bodywork. They might not be human at all, but sparsely so.

What else is odd about the Fourth Dimensional souls is that the inhabitance can manifest at any age in their lives from birth to death; if they think about a certain period of their lives – they are at that age again. If one's mothers feel the remembering their son as a five-year-old to their son's amusement, the son's inner point of light as a kid will overcome the older soul as an adult; he then returns to his original form after his thought is finished. I have heard it before that the souls there as like a time snake from birth to death. It is partly true, but no imagery of a past or future self is seen if not addressed mentally by the self or others. What one seems is like a snake, but it is a grey-blue type of energy to either side of him/her and on top and on the bottom that might not be noticeable if the subject is not surfaced.

There is a misleading YouTube show about *time travel* in the Fourth Dimension. Yes, one can travel back in time in the Fourth to when they met their wife/husband but can alter no events. They cannot meet their past selves and choose a different destiny. All they can do in the past is to understand better the choices made then and try to apply those corrections to their present fluid state. The video mentions that one can choose differently when traveling back in time; the old you would die to give birth to the new you with its new destiny - This is false!

In a fourth dimensional house, one can view all aspects of its sides from inside to outside and everywhere else. To view a fourth dimensional closed Chest, one can see inside of it even if closed. A fourth dimensional doctor can view any organ he wishes to see by deciding to view them. Fourth dimension special travel is instead to thinking about the new location to travel to. It seems like that location comes to the seeker, but what does happen is that one is renewed from the point of light in one's solar plexus to be manifest in that all new location. One looks like he/she disappears and reappears in a new location within the cycle of renewal of the self. One is usually resurrected to a new life and not reincarnated to a new life. The same renewal of the self is performed. If one does not manifest back fast enough, he/she may be renewed to their dimension Astral to expand with negative energies as sweet atoms have been exhausted for them; this I true anywhere not just there. These last few lines describe why we need to die here in the Earth and why souls come down to the Earth: We die to our planet because our sweet atoms are no longer functionable here. Souls come down from the Astral because negative energies no longer feed them. Yes, there are escapist souls in the Astral who are irresponsible. They do not listen to their guides there. They are forced to incarnation after thousands of Earth years. Even the great Sun god Re got old in his astral kingdom of Egyptian life there and had to be reborn as Heru – a human.

This thought raises the question: Is there a present state in the Fourth? The gift of the Third Dimension is the gift of the *present state to experience*, but what about the Fourth? Answer: They have *the present state* in a more fluid form than us. Their current state is arbitrary by the nature of the Fourth. One can only encounter others if they agree on a common present state; otherwise, they are invisible even if they are in the same house or room. Meaning the state of now may not be the state of now to the next person. One needs to be in the mutual state *of the now* as if they are at the threshold of God; this establishes a state of peace, harmony, and unselfish love in their Dimension and associated multiverses it possesses. The Hindus and New Agers try to see the Face of God in each person, but in the long run, the practice fails them all. The New Agers even attempt to put their foes in tiny pink bubbles in the palm of their hands, and with a gentle blow, they are in the golden sunset of God's light. I feel that both visualizations are ungrounded and not a norm in our Dimension. The reason why they both talk like that is due to an overly active Yellow Realm's Mind and believe in a savior principle out of a depressed state of being.

The reason why external foods are needed in physical Realms is because of – Sweet Atoms. Else just energy centers are needed from energy emitting planets in energetic Realms – Astral; this is true in Dimension Three to Five but no higher. No, in energy emitting Astral Realm's growth is not possible – only expansions of what is already. This state in the Astral has an extended stay and is termed as a Pralaya – rest. Our whole Universe disappears and goes into a Pralaya, a state of rest. The matter/energies need to be redesigned to reflect a new and original life unseen before; the two are unrelated.

There are three types of incarnations/resurrections—the species' survival, the Artist, and the Master Architect. The survival of the species is subconsciously and not awakened to true lives. When one reaches the Fifth Dimension to be awakened as the Buddha, one will revisit the older Dimension lives to educated them more the Third to the Fourth. Who knows that our best spirit guide is us ourselves? The Artists' lives serve as a conduit of creative forces that are not of a personal growth of the soul. They are lives of service only. The Architect branch of lives is magical, again a conduit of higher forces to bless the Realm and planets structuring. Many god-kings are of this type, and those who present themselves human sacrifices as well. The latter two categories are Vishnu type of incarnations. For the most part, we incarnate beyond our will in a sleeplike state like the animals do. There is one more category of incarnation: The awaken-self-incarnation. This category is life is Buddha like in its nature but with no service required. They set an evolutionary marker for the race and planet and are usually of very rich and educated. Our passive Illuminati are of this type of life. The active type of Illuminati is of the Master Architect type. They are usually Freemasons and Theosophist.

In the Hindi faith, they call this Dimension - the fourth heaven or Nirvana. The word Nirvana means – blown out; this refers to the oil lamp being blown out at the end of the prayer session as one pain and suffering are blown out with the flame. So, we can see that Nirvana - the Fourth Dimension by having no pains or suffering with no evils of their world. In Nirvana, Moksha is freedom from Samara – Moksha being the cycle of incarnations, and samsara means to the world of desire. So, in this Dimension, we are in our atman body or to say non-self or true self-body. The Brahman consciousness of Universal wisdom and joy is awakened in us. We are at one with the sweet atoms of Universal Joy. The anatta self or non-self has no limits, so universality expresses easily. No, there is no evil or evil souls in the Fourth Dimension. You might ask why? Well, the answer has more to do with the Universal expansion than an honest answer. The sweet atoms are ignited in one soul there, and one can only express Universal joy. Because unhappiness and lack are not present there, we have no bases for evil or exist there.

In this Dimension, we have three sexualities in its lower Realms as we do in ours, but six sexualities in its higher Realm. We have 1-Straight, 2-Homosexual/lesbian with like manner genitals; 3- men with vaginas; 4 females with male genitals; 5- same-sex attracted men with vaginas and last 6- same-sex attracted females with male genitals; even no sexuality in its highest Realms as in the Purple Realm of our Dimension. They seem to possess, and unseen by us, a new primary color that I cannot describe outside of a Fourth Dimensional brain.

That primary color mixed with the three primaries; we know of to create Four new colors. The inhabitance of this Dimension gains their substances like any of our Dimension. Still, it is even more independent from its environment of externals in its even higher Realms than its lower Realms in those multiverses. The number of Multiverses of one Dimension is uncountably high. In its many Red to Yellow Realms of sets of Universes, foods are external to them and grow independently from their efforts in their environment to harvest. In other words – it's out there for the taken with little to no efforts. ' The needed nutrition responds subconsciously to those takers and is available everywhere – even in the sky. Its Red Realm is truly wild with its passions for life and the self there; the self is the key in the Dimension of Three to Five under the one soul design. In its Red Realm most foods are fruits but apart from that its fungi. As for needed nutrition are a concern, their inhabitants use the same model in Dimensions from Three to Five but are more independent from externals in its higher Realms. Eventually, all nutrition is absorbed through their skin at the energy centers like in the Astral in our Dimension in their higher Realms. Yes, in their Yellow Realms, food is harvested as in ours, but without farming or livestock, as the inhabitants are all vegetarians. The eating of meat is only in our early human evolution in their Red Realm.

The majority of Indians in India who are vegetarians are advanced higher than we are. I have met mathematicians in India online. These people are even well versed in quantum and even my theories. Somehow, I feel that eating meat is not good for the use of the Mind's higher rationale abilities. The point about feeding in the Fourth is intuitive harvestings in one's area where they live. There are no cities in the Fourth Dimension, but uncountable small villages are equal in importance, so nutritional finds are reality available in nature. Most of their foods are Fungi. Their spores are embedded in every teaspoon of soil one can find. Instead, growth by request is responsive to the needy one in question.

So, Nirvana is freedom from death? What is death as we know it? Death is the aging process that leads to an untimely end of the incarnation's experiences upon the planet. In the Fourth, it does not exist at all. One is born to the planet and leaves when they need different experiences outside of the incarnated entities' scope. The passing souls go to an intermediate Realm for organizations and education for future lives like in our Dimension. We in our Third Dimension will be like Nirvana in due time with no death. The fact is, only the Fourth Dimension's Red Realm will experience death. In the bulk of the other Realms, just one principal life is used with periodic deaths with resurrections as the same person back to life.

It is quite a shame that sweet atoms are not ignited in our hearts in Astral planes realities anywhere. We are at a disadvantage due to that. One can still express – sweet atoms by opening our hearts to loving with equally in our physical planes of realities. In the Astral planes of energetic realities, negative matter comes to their inhabitance needs for nutrition – not sweet Atoms.

One of our Third Dimensional lessons is – selfless love; this is a qualifying steppingstone to the Fourth Dimension. If one can instill this virtue in our soul in repetitive incarnations as a treat one possesses, the Fourth Dimension may be an option allowed when planning a future life?

So, this Dimension seems to be the place of love and compassion. I feel, comparably to our Dimension, as possibly putting us in the dark. The Fourth is a very Holy place. I think that many Catholic Saints left our Dimension of residence there. I also feel that possibly many souls for there have incarnated as Catholic Saints. That Dimension's higher Realms of souls serves along with our higher Realm's - our Purple Realm - of so-called Angel to assist humanity in their most challenging times. In the Fourth Dimension's higher Realm, they are inter-dimensional. They can even manifest in the physical as space aliens with flying saucers to visit us to monitory our growth and influence our governments to a higher evolutionary path unknown to us.

There are five polytopes' shapes in our Third Dimension, Six shapes in the fourth, four shapes in the fifth, and Three in all higher-ups. Their cells are made from flat polytope objects like flat squares, triangles, pentagons, and hexagons. The edges are put together to create the cells. The total number of perfect cells in our Dimension is six. Any other cells are not unique but a version of lower-valued cells. The Fourth Dimension having six polytopes makes it a field for the highest growth possible. In our Dimension, growth is possible, but more so in the Fourth Dimension. The extra polytope is the key in instilling the *sweet atoms* to the Fourth Dimensional entity and their worlds at large.

The higher we go in the Dimensions; we gain one more primary color per Dimension. A new primary color is unknown in the Fourth Dimension, making many new, colors impossible to imagine, if not in a dream or near-death experience. Such near-death experiences may open us up to higher Dimensions and Realms of our Third just by accident. If open to the Fifth Dimension, one may even see many new colors and even see different mixtures of themselves. We can only idealize the new color by noticing a dark to light dot that flashes between the two in a light blue to dark bronze hue. I am using current references to describe this description when one can use no current references in seeing it. Our dreams are the only way to view them. That is, if we Master Spirit in the Ninth Dimension, wills it so.

The new agers call that master spirit – the higher self. As far as the multi-Realms in this Dimension possess, it has Ten Realms. It uses the same seven as we have in our Dimension plus three more Realms. The two Realm to either end of the primary colored one shows two other colors that cannot be described as it is mixed with the new indescribable color. Above its, Purple is the Realm associated with the new color mixed with the Purple creating yet one of the three unseen colors. Then we have the primary of the unseen color with it mixed with Red, making one follow it that bridging it to its Red Realm. To state it simply, its seven lows are like ours, but of the Fourth Dimension. With every new color we have a new Chakra above us for our growth.

From its Blue Realm upward, the inhabitance gets more Inter-Dimensional and can assist those in need. The highest and most etheric space aliens might be from those Fourth Dimensional Realms. I can say about these Realms of the Fourth with its associated indescribable colors that the inhabitance experiences there is Universally political. Their union of planets is very tight, and they cooperate on a Universal level of joy and happiness. They like to give lower Realm and lower Dimensional Realm presence of love and joy. They try to reach us here on our planet using new religions. Both Het-Heru, Ra and Aset, Debt-het of the Egyptian and Haniel are from there. Both the Buddha and the Christ are from a yet higher Dimension – the Buddhist Dimension of the Fifth. The Krishna Consciousness is the highest consciousness to try to possess and it of the Eight.

There is no real Krishna as there was no Earthly Jesus. The Krishna Consciousness is about the Eight Dimensions energies and is higher than the Christ consciousness, though both are archetypical in their true nature. The two consciousnesses are designed to function as one together. What the two are, is described as Thought Adjusters. We all have our own Thought Adjusters, but from the times from Krishna to Jesus, we are working much closer with these Adjusters in our everyday lives than ever before. Hercules, who grounded the Astrology system of growth, was the first Master to be used as a savior of humanity – then Krishna, the Buddha, and lastly, The Christ. The so-called religious wars of Mohammad's day were for self-defense as they were pacifists. The Poet Mohammad never used violence to spread his words; it was from misinformed future followers of him who did not understand his message at all who used wars and violence to relate to their Allah.

Our Earth mother prefers not to have intelligent life on her body due to her unique energies – the wilds of nature - that are uncooperative with intellectual life. She likes animals, insects, microbes, and plant life only. That is why the age of the dinosaurs last millions of years and we are only a few thousand. Yes, there were the Elohim, but she did not help them develop because they were from Alcyone originally and not of her prodigy. However, she opened a passage to a lower Realm to live in another world away from her while the planet froze. Each Realm of Earth has its own Earth mother. Though all four Earth Mothers are under one fifth Dimension soul as four separate entities with multiple Minds.

The tenth dimensional Lords empower our set of Earth Mothers. The Red Realm's Earth Mother welcomed the Elohim with joy as she needed an intelligent life there. Odd to say, our Yellow Realm is of mental vibration, though – so why? Hum? I think it might be bird life in question then with a yellow hue Realms and intellectual whale and dolphin. I understand that Gaia will only help intelligent life so they can evolve and get away from her. We, too, will be met with the same fate if we overstay our welcome here. However, to begin with, Gaia seems to like us a lot more than the Elohim because we are here a prodigy. Gaia knows our polluting of her body and air will be short-lived.

The Alcyon cultivated were the first humans to live on our planet's early Earth. The vegetation then was Purple and violet – not green as today. Gaia did not like how they did not evolve locally upon the Earth but on a foreign planet. She was cool toward them as they were not her children for her to mother too. We are her children, and she loves us greatly.

The polarity we have to the Fourth makes us lovable and social. It was the only way Gaia would have had us. The Fourth-Dimension polarity does have mixed complications, but a balance between self and non-self is essential to like here. If we do not understand it, only unhappiness and destructive forces will cause mass confusion of races and the whole world. We must learn the balance between the personal and trans-personal self to guarantee our happiness and success here.

Many people say the Fourth Dimension is about time. Time is our Dimension is to host the present moment. In the Fourth, there are many present moments. Their attention is more diverse than our one-pointed use of Mind. Their time is non-linear where our I linear. Time there is subjected to one's needs of it. One can focus on multiple time lots and be there enough to satisfy their needs successfully. Simultaneous motion is not so uncommon to our bodies or Minds, but to the frontal lops of our brains, it is unheard of before.

The brain's frontal lops operate on a superficial level. Both our ego-Mind and our anger-Mind meet at the frontal lops of shallow thinks. Yes, it is true that angry egoistical people are quite shallow-Minded and do not think of the long-term consequences of their actions. Our use of time in our practice is shallow. Time in the Fourth is so much wiser and enriching. One takes into consideration so many variables to come up with the right decision. I recall an angry drag queen who had the impression that I said she wore ass pads. I had to get away from her. In time she saw that I was a gorgeous young guy and wanted to know me. It was beyond me then – no way! Do you see how shallow-Minded anger can be?

Yes, with a much deeper Mind, all outcomes are responsible ones. That is why life is so peaceful there – their deep use of the Mind is much faster than ours. Our emotions are fourth-dimensional by their very nature. Our hearts are the gateway to the Fourth Dimension. If we can get the anger out of our feelings, we might trust it to be a new dimension of Mind. We call this – empathic rationale. Such rationale is rarely spoken about anywhere. Might we not be at that level of progress yet? Anyway, let's consider the following:

What is the rationale for communicating with empathy?

When we have empathy, it means we can understand what a person is feeling in each moment and understand why other people's actions made sense to them. Empathy helps us communicate our ideas in a way that makes sense to others, and it helps us understand others when they communicate with us.

Lastly, very high use of the Mind is one's proper use of the imagination. I am not talking about one's self-delusions to one's self-center false needs, but the meeting of God and experiencing whatever it is to come for it. This use of the Mind is called - Divine imagination, which is one or very few forces in nature that our God can personally approve. Many rear death stories are like this concept as experiences from hours of energetic pray in seclusion are of this Divinity.

The Divine God-Mind is normal to this Dimension in each of it vastly populate multiverses and associated Realms. It is made possible because of their use of a much deeper Mind there with the experiences of multiple now reflecting one vast deep of thought to address, creating a multi-reality in their brains to reflect outward. The closest we come to know this use of the Mind is termed at the Higher Mind, which is capitalized. We can only access this state occasionally in life, but its constant access is in the Fourth. In the Secret Doctrine by H.P Blavatsky in 1880, she wrote about the *Antahkarana*, the rainbow bridge; this is a point in the brain where one crosses to access their higher facilities use the Mind.

According to numerology, the number four represents the forces of nature. What many superstitious folks call the little people of our

Orange Realms just might not be them at all but projected fairies from fourth-dimensional intelligence to help humanity. The Fae folk may seem very likable and natural to us, but they are a non-living entity. After their work is done, they fade away. Many orphan children have been raised by their Faery Mothers only to learn one day that they were never real at all.

The driving forces of nature in our Dimension stem from the fourth. The effect is heightened for in our planet's natural park. One day we all would leave our world to let it evolve according to nature. In two thousand years, there will be no evidence that humans were living on Earth. All will be green with oceans full of fish with wildlife of all kinds living with no threat from man. In most fourth dimensional planets nature comes first to progress. To live with nature is very fourth dimensional.

The numbers 4 and 22 are vibrating in this Dimension, creating the power of structure like a very well-built building like the Pantheon of Rome or the Great Pyramids of Gaza, Egypt. Personal independent understanding is easy here in this Dimension as the number 22/4 is a Master number of initiations to higher growths and realities. One can say that they truly know themselves in the Fourth. However, the fifth will break through the tight ego structures of the Fourth. The Fourth is where one becomes a healthy Ego and is said to where true living and life begins. The riddle of the Fifth Dimension is acquiring a transpersonal life while driving further into self-understanding. That sound counter intuitive but is self-evident that the higher Mind is at work in the fifth like nowhere before it. We will dive all of these points as much as possible. I close this chapter about the Fourth Dimension with regret that I do not understand it better. I hope what I have written already is helpful enough. The material will only get more abstract from here on; please give it a slow but steady read. OM

Chapter 11

The Fifth Dimension

This Dimension with its thirteen Realms has yet one more unseen primary color and is the domain of the Buddhas. The Christ, the Buddha, and many archetypical Gods/Goddesses reside there. This domain is also known as the – *split personalities* Dimension. One's soul is fragmented into as many selves as needed to acquaint oneself closer to their leading soul. Another name for this domain is – *the soulmate* Dimension. Yet, another name might be – the Dimension of *alternative possibilities?* We shall go into each category using three parts of this chapter. There are thirty-two points in this five-dimensional cube of the Fifth. Like the Fourth-Dimension's cube that renews itself in a cycle, the cycle itself takes on duplication and renews itself in multiple versions of its original self - so, the - I, becomes the – We! The observer dictates the number of multiples and, to add, how these multiples appear; this is an arbitrary Dimension with arbitrary lives, objects, and Universes holding many worlds; We use this very principle in our universal unfolding in universal clusters in our Third Dimension. The law used stems from our Fifth Dimension. All Dimension affects each other, so higher dimensional rules are not uncommon to hear of it.

We need the Fifth Dimension to unite gravity and electromagnetism as one force in our dimensional Universe. This Dimension's size is a 10^{-33} cm loop. In the multi-dimensional Multiverse worlds of the Fifth, it is scarce, if ever, that any non-soulmate connections occur. We are constantly encountering ourselves in that world. A YouTube show mentioned that these selves are in different Universes, but the show is wrong, as such a phenomenon is of the Sixth Dimension alone.

There is just a heavy gravity between the multi-selves to be so far apart in separate realities. As seen in the thirty-two-pointed cube, it seems tight. A sixth-Dimensional cube reaches different realities unseen by the original cube. We may ask: What is a soulmate anyway? It is *You* but seen and encountered with other bodies and Minds between them all.

So, the new vector is I & We. Though, in the Sixth it – We & Them. In the Seventh, it is the – the trueness of the I amongst them all. After the Six Dimension, we are narrowing more into finding the true –of the I. In the Eight, we have the - I in respect to God as the multiples of the - I – spirit, where no physical and spiritual bodies are found – it's the Dimension of pure Mind in the Eight Dimension. In the Ninth Dimension, we see the Master I- the spirit of God, but still as an Egoist force. The Egoic forces have two levels 1 – the free-ranged soul 2- the free-ranged spirit. These Ranges are the rebellious fields under the Tenth Dimension. From the Tenth upward, one cooperates with the hand of God in the making of all peace and warm loving everywhere.

This Dimension is termed the soulmate Dimension since we are constantly encountering versions of ourselves there. There is no master-self as in split personalities managers but an over-seeing soul housed in the Seventh Dimension and a Master Spirit housed in the Ninth Dimension. One indeed can be in love with one's real soulmate there and have true friends. The only occasion that these unions are negative is when a profound unknown aspect of the soul would need to emerge. If such inter-reactions are not peaceful, the elements of the selves may need a few fourth or third-dimensional incarnations to work the issue out. There may still be cohesive unions in different aspects of the soul still inter-reaction simultaneously in the Fifth Dimension, while a particular isolated element of the soul is working matters out in the Lower Dimension in their associated Multiverses of worlds.

Yes, one does need volunteers from the lower Dimensions Astral Realm to inter-react and represent the pros and cons of the issue at hand to be worked out. I feel that it may take many Earth years to recruit such volunteers. If the Jiva is evolved enough to be of the Fifth, most of His soul family tribe might be so with him in his Dimensional reality. Yes, it will be a get-to-know-you challenge in finding these recruits in the Astral to battle with one. These issues of non-integration of the soul and spirit can happen on even higher levels, up to the Ninth Dimension. After the Ninth, we are freed from the battlefield, so to say.

Time travel is easier in the Fifth than the Fourth. One can just go back in time to adjust and error to attune to a finer present. Such attunements will create a new destiny line, though. The original will still be as it is, unfortunate. Only in the Sixth Dimension can we truly have many destinies. The Fifth Dimension has many imperfect remnants of bad timelines to be cleaned up in the Sixth Dimension. Bilocation is also possible in the Firth in one's Multiverse only. There is no inter- Dimension travel unless an arranged plan of incarnations as explained above by one master spirit who lives in the Ninth.

This Dimension is also known as the Buddhi domain. The Buddha and the Christ both originated in the Fifth. The Buddha had a physical incarnation, but Christ only had a Purple Realm to our Third incarnation to work with Shamballa's government to manage a consciousness over the Earth of His Christ-like character. The Christ consciousness truly is the union of all of God's sons at once as a group soul. This consciousness was devised to speed up the spiritual and intellectual progress of the Western World on planet Earth. The Buddha's work had to be achieved in the flesh, being that he had to ground to his Earth many doctrines of the East's education. Lord Krishna from the Eight Dimension had an incarnation like the Christ – in the Purple Realm to influence the Indian peoples and inspire them to be beautiful and insightfully spiritual doctrines.

It's best not to comment on the Muslim faith or Muhammad's credibility as it might be taken as controversial. However, the original words of the prophet – the 144 Surahs, are holy. The contributing doctrines - The Habit, written after the prophet's death, are not in line with his holiness. Both original works – the 144 Surahs that Muhammad received from the Archangel Gabriel and later worked - the Habit, written by later followers are known today as the Quran or Koran – recitation in English. The latter works – Habith and the 144 Surahs may be misinterpreted and possibly lead to Muslim violence as we know it today. One might say that even Muhammad is of the Fifth Dimension, but anyone's insights are not too sure of that fact.

In my research in the Fifth Dimension with its associated Multiverses, we find us in Realms of multi-possibilities, regarding causations holding multiply affects. A living soul is causation, as he/she is vulnerable to specific reactions. In this Dimension, singular causation may have multiplied responses that need their fields of expansions – realities; this is truly a center of the Universe soul experience reality in the Firth. There is only you there! No one else exists but you! all our encounters are self-encounter involving multiple – Us! Yes, there are other souls there too, but you rarely inter-react with them on any level of depth. I say the reality of an individual alone, about the self's meaningful inter encounters. I wonder if it's the same way here. There can be questioned by us never connecting with specific individuals. In our reality, it's for Karmic reasons for the most part. In the Fifth, Karma is inter-personal and does not involve others.

There is yet one more primary color shading that Dimension's multi-Realm worlds. They have five primary colors that mix into Twenty-one colors from five primaries. The Fourth has thirteen colors from four primaries. We have seven colors. However, indigo is a mixture of purple/blue, and we may not truly consider it a color. We do just the same, according to a mathematical law unknown. The math is primary = $(N^2) - N + (1)$. So, in the Sixth Dimension we have $6^2=36 - 6 + 1 = 31$ colors. The highest primary loops with the base primary create a new mixed color and a mixed one to the lower primary. In the Seventh, we have forty-three colors for seven primary colors. After the Seventh Dimension, colors do not exist. The Eight is the mother of both matter and energy to say spirit and the physical as one ray of substance we lost in words for, but he called – The Universal Mind! This Dimension governs the lower seven but stands apart from them. The higher band of this Dimension is dynamic, while its lower is passive and the holds power in its middle band. A is in chapter dedication to its explanations. So, please read on!

We can even have sex with ourselves in this Dimension. One truly gets to know themselves in a profound manner unexplainable. The depths of the self-knowledge one can gain there is so deep it would both scare and embarrass us. The understanding of solitude is better known in the Fifth. Oddly, I am saying this, see that self-inter-reactions are paramount there. Souls learn solitude after eons of growth in the Fifth. The Fifth is like a Monastery with just one person in it. That one person is reflected in many others to encounter and to get to understand each other. As one comes to know themselves, these – other selves seem to come less and less until you are of the master self. The solitude master self is the primary goal of this Dimension. Considering our Eighth Dimensional theme - as to know God by trying to be Him, we instill the sense of being a self-made God soul awareness beyond any doubt or self-questionings. We learn to be God and to stand apart in our satisfaction with this position we will take.

There is a Buddhist nature to this Dimension. The Buddha can recall all of his past lives from humans, animals, fish, inspects, elementals, spirits, and beyond to his credits of self-knowledge, just like the Buddha was able to recall all his past existences.

The idea of multi lives in recognition of being the same person is hard to understand. The understanding is more like meeting an old friend to recall their mutual past in their old town. How would it be like to meet the other forms yourself? It is a sense of the overwhelming familiarity of oneness one feels but is still holding to their position on that mutual understanding. But can one of these simultaneous selves be in another Universe? If so, they are a branch monad/Mind of the self to work out pacific values until all a reduction of the self in just one Universe.

The notion of the Monadic self was metaphysical and only learned from 1970 to late 1990 before the internet closed any new aged shopping to the superficial. The Golden Age of math shortly after had reopened it in a must grander manner of studies. Yet, the Monadic self is not known. What this is, is an aspect of the larger whole of the self. Monad means Oneness, so one soul is divided into fragments yet still atone, but its Mind is the fragmented part – no, the soul. So, an aspect of the self can branch off the needed alternative environments to work its self-understandings required before its final reunion.

The Buddha, Christ, and other incarnations of Vishnu are godlike. They come, for the most part, from the Fifth to help humanity progress. This service is a needed initiation before such souls are then fragmented into multi-souls in the Sixth Dimension. In other words, to lose a unique soul, one must be a complete soul first. We are not faithful souls until we develop in the Fifth Dimension. In the Fourth, we know our hearts; in our Dimension, we know our Egos as a full-blown Ego even if seen by others as ridiculous. Being a stupid full-blown Ego is our Dharma here to achieve and to get over it leave it behind. Our Fourth Dimensional polarity may inhibit this process due to humility. I say no that all size is relative to the Mind of the soul and its needs. One can be significant but seem small to others.

The vibration of the number five is of a blue hue. This Dimensions blue Realm holds the most significant fields of growth there as it is doubly blue in a vibrational hue. Our yellow Realm is doubly Yellow as the Third Dimension has a yellow vibration hue to it to begin. Our Minds will develop on a mastering level in due time upon our Earth and other planets we may incarnate to in the future. Our Earthly commitment will primarily retain us to the Earth in our incarnation, though. We are meant to have this plan from our Earth mother as she will us to progress directly to the Fourth Dimension by the time our Earth heats up and can no lone host life here. Yes, we shall all die as a planet, but our destiny is far more progressive than all our neighboring solar systems hosting advanced intelligent life. There are even angelic so-called being who are jealous of our destiny and refuses to help us even though they can. I read that these souls are not angelic, but to my knowledge, they are physical and not too far from us in our galaxy.

The written works of the Buddha are literature I strongly recommend, along with Hindu text as well. The esoteric non-religious Christ consciousness learned from the alternative spirituality communities is my third recommendation. Rudolf Steiner seems to handle all these three faiths skillfully and intellectually. I know this from my many years living in New York City, where the Steiner Institute is located.

Lastly, I state that one life purpose is brought out fully in the Fifth Dimension. One can realize and answer the many riddles of life far deeper than anywhere in the lower realities. Such is our awakening to the Buddha Consciousness. The Buddha teaches that the search for God is not reaching God, ourselves, but the path itself. The many highs and lows are the meaning of life itself. God's essence is life. So, if we reach God, that would be the end of all life; this cannot happen, so we are never to meet our God but left to search for evermore. In His love for us, God has blessed the Seventh Dimension for us to find the right God proxy satisfying our needs for one, though. In the truest sense, we meet with God enough to ignite our spirits to a more satisfying life orientation; this can only be made possible if a spiritual direction is needed first.

In the next chapter, we will learn how and how why our soul will be fragmented into multiple souls to gain the most profound self-knowledge on a spirit level and not just on a soul level. After reading the next chapter, who knows, you might take our wishes of being Elves Presley or Marilyn Monroe seriously? If our spirit, will it? Who knows? The question remains: We might have soul knowledge, but do we have a spiritual understanding of regarding ourselves in the grandest scheme of all life? Most would say – Not at all. In the Six, we have our first spirit encounters. The truth is, at our level of growth, our spirits are foreign to us. The Six Dimension will open the familiarity to our spirit's wills and wishes.

Chapter 12

The Sixth Dimension

The Dimension of the multi-soul

I n no other written literature has it been reported that we have multiple spirits and souls. This phenomenon occurs in the Sixth Dimensions. Likewise, we have various spirits in the Eighth Dimension. For our sense of orientation, we need to discuss what exactly is a Soul and a Spirit?

A Soul reflects a misunderstanding from the physical Universe of both energy and matter. We need to overcome these misunderstandings to enter the Seventh Dimension of so-called heavenly and earthly paradises. A Spirit must project itself downward to lower realities of the Eighth Dimension to the First to obtain a soul. Our first soul's misunderstanding pertains to our theme of our One to Eight set reality of Dimensions: *to try to understand God by trying to be Him.* Already, this is absurd and gives reason for such misunderstandings; thus, resulting in creating a primitive soul. The soul comes to know its absurdity further in higher Dimensions in the fullest possible way; one needs to do this to 1- see the absurdity for what it is, and 2 – to release such folly.

Only in the Seventh Dimension is this possible to see and release this folly. There, we will have a perfected soul and come to understand those follies in a way unknown to us currently. Those insights are empirically obtained, personal, and is relative to the individual soul. It would be fool hearty if I shall indicate even one aspect of this insight of self-perfections. Many Catholic saints have written about their perfections of the soul. Please, do not read them, as they are uniquely relative to those individuals, and they would misguide us by individual inspires unrelated to one's unique individual by writing those writings.

In many New Aged books, they call the soul an ego. The ego has a tight identity with self-defended boundaries to its entity. A soul has what we call – a self-consciousness, but so does a Spirit up to the Twelfth Dimension. However, the soul's self-consciousness retains a separate body entity when the Spirit shares a mutually shared body reflecting nonmaterial values. We will discuss the nature of the Spirit first in the fourteen and fifteenth chapters, where we find multiple spirits selves present. For now, the soul's nature is independence from God and anything that we may call sanity.

The soul is insanity itself. To say one has soulful eyes implies being sympathetic and sincere. They are usually referring to responding to one trouble. So, we see that problems are implied. Soulful eyes need troubles to reflect; else, they will not be recognized. What is a Spirit? To understand the Spirit, we need a brief essay on the Ninth Dimension on which it is based. The Ninth Dimension is of a passive form of the mother of both matter and energy - Mulapakriti. The nature of the Spirit is a passive, attractive force of a vortex with a substance that is hard to explain. There are stringed loops created in the Tenth Dimension to offer some form of substance for spirits one Dimension below.

This vortex of passive string loops is polarized as negative to set its ways to lower Dimensional experiences with associated multiverses. In the Tenth Dimension, the forces are balanced with no lower polarities. I have dedicated a chapter to the Ninth to Twelfth Dimensions in explaining the nature of – Mulapakriti. From my writing so far, we can see that the Spirit is designed for lower reality experiences. It is a vortex of light substance with a naïve consciousness to lower reality experience as it stands apart from them. The Spirit may or may not descend downward to take up absurd notions of God's nature or not. The Spirit has a Universal consciousness and is subconscious to live here. Our spirits can only affect the subconscious. Its effect is primarily to do the work! The Spirit is not a noun but a verb; it does not have, it just is beings; have no values, it just wants to empower you to find our peace; it is not a concern with God's riddles but still want to better it loves with God. This only ailment is having allows us to seek it solutions in the lower realities. It is not until the Thirteenth Dimension that consciousness is eradicated as we know it.

The Spirit does not have a consciousness of its own yet is akin to the heavenly rebellion for its source, which fuels Mulapakriti itself. This Spirit is the rebellious Lucifer. Lucifer was upset because he couldn't get closer to God. His feud with God was over humanity, not appreciating God enough. So, Lucifer misleads them into rebellion and their fall from grace. One-third of the sons of God followed Lucifer and became instigators of trouble. They were still angelic but has made separate from God. The Spirit is the affirmation of such rebellion from our source. The Spirit felt that it killed God to be him and gain our self-consciousness as a soul, which fuels all reactions we call – evil! Yet again, I state that the Spirit addressing itself to lower realities is trying to work out this riddle of getting loved by God more is possible.

This soul is fragmented into multiple reflections of its original nature due to a law of advanced quantum unknown to us that states a duality. The Fifth Dimension influences this duality by causing the duality to form multiple versions of the Soul Mind. The soul twins of the Fifth Dimension are at work to emerge yet more unknown desires forgotten or never unearthed. The astrological sign or Gemini explains it nature. The two Greek gods helped shipwrecked sailors and brought favorable winds for those who made sacrifices to them. Their mother was Leda. Castor was the mortal son of Tyndareus, the king of Sparta, and Pollux, the demigod son of Zeus, who seduced Leda in the form of a swan. One of our twin souls knows our divinity with our source – God; the other feels in need to find its divinity as if it needs to be earned and evolved into by an evolutionary process.

A Sixth Dimensional sphere looks like an American football with two spinning hearts to either side with their apex facing outside. There is a fragile central tube that pierces the football at a long angle. The Gravity is very faint, but it is felt very strongly in holding the sphere together. This sphere opens a mystery of Gravity that changes its rules in higher Dimensions. The structure alone dictates the Gravity, but why does such a weak gravity hold the structure may be understood? Answer: The central axis tube is the main structure of the sphere, but the neutral Gravity it possesses keeps that tube as it is. Neutral Gravity is first seen in Fourth with Dynamic Gravity. We, in our Dimension, only have passive negative Gravity. From the Fourth to the Fifth, we start seeing both dynamic, positive Gravity and neutral Gravity, but it is weak but more potent in the Fifth. The three gravities are equal and present in the Sixth Dimension. This neutral Gravity is the key to all structures in the Sixth.

The Six-Dimensional cubes have more faces than the Fifth does, but with a mysterious quality. I will explain now how both energy and matter to change in the values of the observer. When one observes a Six-Dimension soul or anything there, it multiplies to the wishes of the observer. The observer, in our case, is primarily our spirits. We can be fragmented further by the inter - reaction if ignited either in a good or bad way. I have said that this is the Elves Presley and Marylyn Monroe Dimension earlier. The truth is, if we Spirit feels that we cannot continue unless we might be a rock star or a sex bomb in a Three-Dimensional world, we will have to be that person. A unique soul would manifest in the right reality do just that. The Sixth Dimension has a very heavy Third Dimensional polarity as seen in its sphere with the two three-Dimension hearts to either side of the football. Just like the Fourth has a second-Dimensional polarity and the fifth a Ten and First-Dimensional polarity.

The Seventh has no polarity to it at all to lead to possible incarnations. In this Dimension, our souls are multiplied into a vast number of souls directed in their multiverses to fit their desires of set understandings. The level of consciousness of the Sixth, the vibration of the Sixth, has one been more responsible to their inner mysteries of who they are with the lust of life to be just about anything possible to be and have. Leisure is akin to the sixth as well. So, all experiences are handled non-serious leisurely; as if they say: if I only had the chance to do it over again, I would not be as serious as before. When one is open and loses, Spirit can enter far more freely, bringing more satisfying results. When one gives life a second chance, as in the Sixth in its lower reality directives, one is usually passive and more open to the lighter aspects of life than in the first round when we are overly serious. The happy types are the revisited souls from the Sixth Dimension.

Do you have a hidden dream to be a star in the Third Dimension? There is a law of karma that all desires must be fulfilled or transmuted to higher desires. Karma is not truly eradicated until we enter Thirteen, where no known consciousness is experienced as we know it.

Back to the Gemini story of Caster - *mortal* and Pollux - *Immortal*, this poses our Dimensional set's theme as looking for one's immortality as an unneeded endeavor; when our divinity is beyond any question that makes our Dimensional set's theme a to be a folly. The question of the real to the unreal is asked in this Dimension. The twins oversee lost sailors because, if sacrifice is made to them, their way will be found; this means that if we question what is real to what is unreal more, we will find our way to true happiness.

If one is to be created as a Marilyn Monroe, it can only be facilitated if the question is challenged. Is it really a reality or a falsehood to be a sex bomb in our Dimension's worlds? How is reality or deception being questioned in their endeavor in the Sixth? Their divine Spirit can only resolve the answer in the Ninth. When one says: Only God knows. What they mean is our Godhead – Spirit. Now, the Seventh Dimensional Lords can be of service. When the question of reality is brought to the Minds of the soul, we are then in the care of our divine spirit arrangers – our Master Spirits. They give such duties of incarnations designs to the Seventh Dimensional administrators by their lower Realms of the Seventh. When such divinity can be arranged, life is usually glamorous and graceful. Who is to say if such a soul is in the question of reality or not? When reality is not questioned, mundane proceeds to small rewards. Questioning life/reality can bring depression in one life. One's creativity is found to be helpful. Marilyn Monroe was very sad in her life, as we all know. Questioning reality is rewarding, but it does have its difficulties too.

In our first round in the lower dimensions, we try far too hard, and we are at a disadvantage in opening to higher inspirations. We are underdeveloped as well as soul, too. When we revisit, we are far more experienced in life, and much more open to higher influences from above – in other words, more successful. Many advanced souls to bless our planet were either from the sixth or in the question of reality. So, who is to say that the soul in question needs a Marilyn sex bomb incarnation? Only our spirits, who permit such a life now. The logic of the Spirit is outside of our human Minds knowing possibly.

The Mind's limit is the Eight Dimension, so beyond it, it is impossible to understand. Such an incarnation cannot be questioned as authentic or not to us lower life forms. One thing I can say is that life's satisfactions are an indication of this question. Our own Marilyn died unhappy and disillusioned. Obviously, apart from being a sex bomb and loved by her public, she found out what truly matters in her life? Some intuitive people say that Marilyn was an ugly nurse in many past lives here on Earth. She built up so much good karma; the Lords in the Seventh designed Marilyn to receive her rewards as a Diva on the big screen. She couldn't accept such a love personality in romance, so she took her own life in time. Being a Diva was not enough – she wanted romantic love.

The Third-Dimension value of special love was brought forward. Apart from Marilyn, if the higher Lord feels that we need such an experience, it might be arranged with a new soul's destiny of a unique character apart from the other souls you have. So true with Elves, George Washington, Julius Caesar, or any tremendous egos legend to be seen. One might think it is odd that we have multiple souls. The truth is – in the Now, have them all now! We are on many Dimensions at the same time to a greater or lesser degree than we know. Though we can only focus on the current soul under the Six, who is to say if other branches of our souls exist in other realities? The answer is Yes - there are.

We will never be able to meet them like in the Fifth's multi-selves as in the Sixth Dimension; life takes on a Dimension far too abstract for most humans to comprehend. The Seventh and The Eighth Dimensions will only lead themselves to vague, abstract reasoning. Metaphors and poetry might be the only means of understanding them. There is a practical use of Poetry if written the right way. Far too many Poets have no idea of what Poetry is meant to be or what it is? The same with metaphorical stories, too – very few know how to write them. Back to the question of what is real or unreal, many souls leave our set of One to Eight Dimensions understanding that its theme of knowing God by being Him is absurd. Spirits may choose other more logical themes or come to pure sanity and return to their origins with the Divine – God. Does the choice return make the Seventh Dimensional heavenly paradise a pigs heaven fool gold find? The over Spirit is in charge if one continues to the Seventh or goes to very high realities or to pure love with God to live out a life according to His logic.

What is real and what is unreal is relative to the needs of the observer. The resolution is not to have- - requirements! God has no needs at all; to be real is Godlike. We need to get beyond our experience needs in questioning God's nature. This idea is the conclusion that many accept in the Six that causes an exit and entrance to pure sanity; this is impossible in our reality. The Six Dimension best facilitates such exist and return to sanity. I ask us to live in a basic manner, but if we have big dreams, perhaps we must accomplish them to get over them and understand them as unneeded or to say unreal. That is the rule of all karma – 1- get it to get over it or 2- rise above it.

Chapter 13

The Seventh Dimension

The Domains of the godheads and its
Fool's Gold paradises heavens lost

Only through the logic of God, apart from any use of mathematics, can we employ true Heaven and paradise. The Seventh Dimension is far from a perfected state as God deems it to be. However, it serves as the perfections of the soul for us, though God sees these perfections as fool's perfections. So, how can it be made perfect for us? There are no corrections of making perfect what is imperfect in God's logic. A lie can never be made valid by changing it around. The soul's perfection is only perfect by our insistence on making the Seventh Dimension real and perfect for us. We seem to need such validations of perfections to structure our soul's bodies. Without the Seventh Dimension's calling for the perfected embodiments of the soul, the soul could never have a structured, or they say, usable body.

Our Master Spirit approves of such follies of such an illogical soul because it needs to assert itself to chain its reality - as being perfect for existence. It does not have the eighth-Dimensional Thought Adjuster employed in full to rectify such folly to be what reality truly is. We, too, also have inefficient use of our Thought Adjuster ourselves. We insist on using this Adjuster for validating our current realities and not seeking much higher and further into the unknown. You might think that in the seventh Heaven, we would be of such a higher Mind? No! We continue to make our follies real as in our false heavens and physical paradises on its many levels or reality – in its Realms.

I mentioned that there are no descending polarities in the Seventh Dimension. The physical paradises and false heavens are of that Dimension but may respond as a third-Dimensional reality. The Red Realm of the Seventh can be employed as a quasi-physical Realm just like its Blue to Purple Realms may be used as heavenly Realms. The Sevenths Blue Realm heaven reflected down to us is a more friendly version of the wild Red Realm of the Seventh Dimension. The Astral of the Seventh is Heaven, and their physical realms are paradises. The Purple Realm is more so what we might call Heaven than anywhere else. We need to use such a Dimension to finish our Dharma – set business; we came into this set of One to Eight Dimensions before seeing through its theme of the Eighth Dimension. The rule is: We must have it to release it. When we release it, we will be fully able to see the false theme of this set - getting to know God better by trying to be Him ourselves.

The sweet atoms of the Universes are feeding in to create a central power of axes that see through all our creations to function: our bodies, planets, Sun, Galaxies, Universes, Universal clusters, and beyond. The sweet atom is not just for one Universe, but from the collective of uncountable Universes to infuse to this central axes of perfections. That is why our reality works too well. True, the Holy Spirit is the secondary driving force to guarantee its success.

That Dimension is what we call the soul's perfections. No longer do we have multiple souls, as seen in the Sixth Dimension. One is the Master Soul in that Dimension of all souls. From here on, the entity is more and more refined in a more simplified manner. There is just one life the master souls have in this Dimension. One soul may change its persona and physical body to suit unique experiences in His reality in the Seventh. They call this the resting place in many spiritual books. One reaps the rewards of their evolution in the Seventh to receive Universal love enough and perhaps be able to unite with the true sanity of God and be with Him to live a reality what God deems real.

All reality that we have come to understand is not seen as sane or real in God's eyes.

Many Catholic Saints have written regarding their perspectives of what their perfections of their souls mean to them. I did mention earlier that to read them might be misleading in finding our inner perfections. Though, they might be a good read to inspire our internal inspirational writings regarding our self-perfection of our souls. Doing so from a third-Dimensional perspective might be encouraged; however, to be a so-called perfect soul can only come when it is ready, and who knows what it may be from our perspectives? We can only elude vaguely in our personal writing's dedication to our self-perfections. Oddly enough, our faithful, God will never recognize our perfections to be in His standards. No Pope of Rome or Dalai Lama of Nepal and Tibet is perfect in God's eye, or does He recognize them to be His true messengers.

This Dimension governs the laws of physics for the six lower Dimensions and monitors and controls their life force. So, the Seventh Dimension serves as a central axis of the group of seven dimensions as a higher Mind level abstraction. Our Third Dimension serves as a second ax in some concrete – lower Mind level manner. The Eight Dimension has its hand in our set of seven Dimension in both higher and lower Mind fields, being that the Eighth is the roots of what we call Mind itself.

The Eight Dimension is the mother of both the physical and energetic. She stands apart from both as a unique element hard to describe apart from calling it – Mind, or the Universal Mind, or Universal consciousness. No matter what universal soul is considered, the Eighth Dimension's Mind embodies them all. So, we can say that the Seventh Dimension is our higher Mind under the umbrella of the Eighth Dimension's thought Adjusters. Our Third Dimension is its lower Mind. How are the two Minds different? The Seventh is only concerned with the growth of the soul's perfections of itself. The eighth has a larger picture of life beyond such silly perfections to a truly impersonal model. We can now see that the Seventh Dimension is concerned with personal perfection and the eighth a more universally impersonal perfection.

Talking about the so-called imbecile's Heaven in the Seventh is very similar to that represented by the religious writer. We have the presence of God felt for the first time as never felt before in the lower six Dimensions. This presence is the real touch that our source makes with souls. Some New Aged books say that God cannot enter our realities to change them, being that He is the author of those realities; this is true, but His presence is first felt there for us to reach His sanity and join His wonderful unknown Mind.

You might wonder why His presence is first felt in the Seventh and not in the lower Dimension? The answer is more of a mathematical one than a logical one. God's presence is felt in all variants of the number seven, ex: 14, 21, 28. The Twenty-Eighth Dimension is the last visit with God before we join Him in Dimension from Thirty to Thirty-Three. Higher Dimension has its chapter – so read on.

Now, what is a Physical Paradise in the Seventh Dimension? The physical planets there are seventh dimensional, but they respond as Three Dimension or even Fourth, or fifth-Dimensional realities depending on the needs of the individuals. Their Heavens are in like manner the same, but Astral/Energetic. The reason for both is to permit the love of God to release them for the hold of this bad dream where they are.

It just might be a comfort to us that our God has arranged for us to meet a qualifying proxy of Himself to encourage and orientate us on our path to nowhere. Such encouragements are needed as the vast path to an unknowable God could have dark areas and uncertainties.

The path is very dark. Our proxy God will enlighten our steps and help us not be so afraid of the darkness in searching for God.

At last, I say that this Dimension is a seat governing all life of the lower Dimension and their environments. The Bible even speaks of the seventh Heaven of God as His government. The number seven is a holy number in numerology that helps us be the superstar we are by revealing our shadow side for its healings. I did mention Shamballa as our world government, but there is a higher authority over that. The Mormon God lives on the Seventh. This godhead negotiated with the Earth mother of the Yellow Realm – our Realm to repopulate human life again after it died over six Million years earlier. This Dimension is the godhead Lord's domains in its many Realms and heavens and physical planes it possesses. This Dimension is like a beauty pageant. All the many souls are presented before a proxy God to judge them. No one wins, but the proxy God knows what he wants to create the master soul.

The master soul is made manifest, but still holds in she grown the many souls that contributed to her success. Even in the Miss America pageant, they are trying to systematically an archetype of a young American Girl. Now, this same pageant is performed on a much grander and elite version of the Ninth Dimension. It is not a lunar beauty sought after but of a solar grandeur that a world leader might be called the presidential election. Even a few New Aged books mentioned that we require the perfections of our souls just enough to give us the essence over to the Divine. Even odd religious cults like the Jehovah's witnesses preach of a paradise Earth with a heavenly government over it. We need the Seventh perfections to regulate our bodies, and all we use to work perfectly enough to be able to serve us.

This reality is far from the perfections of God, but fine enough as a meeting ground for us to encounter a proxy God to orient us on our path. The Lords of the seventh walk as living gods in their rights and serve as the godheads to humanity in hearing their prayer and answering them with love. These godheads there love to make lower realities inhabitance happy and joyous. They are very musical and help composers create symphonies of delights. To understand these Lords is to compose melodic sheet music of the higher spheres. In this Dimension, we first hear true universal melodies unknown to man. We try to write music at their level, but it's impossible. Once we are there, we gain our first taste of Divinity.

Chapter 14

The Eighth Dimension the Mind and the Thought Adjuster

The Eighth Dimension is the domain of the high Lord Krishna. Krishna is the archetype for our Thought Adjusters. One that lives in the Dimension is called – Mind. Mind is the mother of both matter and energy and is neither, but an element on its own. This Dimension has no Realm for the soul's inhabitations, but it hosts spirits inhabitations. Odd phenomena occur in this Dimension, which is the fragmentations of the Spirit in many spirit selves. Each Spirit possesses its destiny apart from the other spirits in its fragmented form. Each spirit branch follows a new and different God theme. There are an uncountable number of these themes for a new spirit branch to choose from. We are subjected to our theme, making it impossible to imagine other themes pertaining to knowing God better in different ways.

The Earth orbits the Sun eight times to fill a thirteen-time Venus/Sun orbit with a shift of 144 degrees. There is an eighth/thirteenth-dimensional agreement between the two plants; this opens our eighth-dimensional Minds to the Universal subconscious if accessed. We still have our ego cut back its Divine magic, though. Our sixth and ninth-dimensional egos create major consciousness flows in our beingness. It would take years of meditations to relax their holds on us, and even so, our bodies are another manifestation of ego blockage. We can only acquire a quasi-sense of its higher divinity. Even if small, it does bless our lives, though in ways we are not aware of in a body. The 144-degree shift sets our total chakras at 144,000, stemming from the seven main ones.

Our Thought Adjuster is the same, no matter what branch of the fragmented Spirit he propagates. This Adjuster is the unifying principle amongst them all. One's Thought Adjuster is an aspect of their Monad – the original oneness. Our Monad is still subjected to its first Dimensional – oneness, but separate oneness body; this gives the Monad some form of an archaic body – separate, but its very nature reflects the Divine in its sad captivity of consciousness. In the Thirteen Dimension, one loses consciousness to the - subconsciousness of God. The Monad and its Thought Adjuster are conscious and not in the most meaningful sense to be deemed true, Divine. For each new Spirit's destiny, its downward branching into the lower seven Dimensions.

There are many new multiverses of new universal experiences to work out its new God-related theme. The cycle ends when either the theme has exhausted itself, or one sees through it; that day will have to come on its own. One's new stay as a spirit branch may be very short of many trillions of Earth's years. Many more Universes will come and go before one's awakening to their end or take up a new theme, of knowing God in a new and different way, or end the Jiva cycle. The infinity sign is a sideways number eight. Infinity is in question here; I will recap my views in this eighth-Dimensional infinity now. To do so, we must consider calculus with it (i) and (p) – (i) being an imaginary number and (p) as potential. We now have an imaginary potentially infinite number of Universes of experience. The p is infinite in that these Universes are reborn differently each time they resurface, making the variety of new Universes amongst a finite number – infinitely renewed. So, it's the renewal of those finite number Universes to be infinite. The p makes it infinite, not the I.

This pattern of energy is what fragments the one Spirit to many the many spirits. This pattern makes the Eighth Dimension quite mathematical. This Dimension is the foundation and planning fields of all branch's spirits descent down into lower uncountable

Dimensions and multiverses to be possible. The obvious answer to all these God-knowing themes is understood well in the Mind's field of this Dimension. What makes one not agree with that answer to these themes is due to the vibrational patterns of this Dimension. The Dimension seems to make it hard for one to adhere to its sanity, but encourages us to take up other ways to know God uses other branch themes to descend into lower reality to resolve.

One might ask: Can a spirit reunite with God at any given point in its journey? Yes, one can! Though they would be sent through Dimensions from Nine to Thirteen to lose one enjoyed body and be open to the subconsciousness of God. Funny thing to say, but I have written that our conscious Minds have nothing to do with God, and it is atheistic. I also meant the studies of divinity to be falsely studied by this Mind! I have said before; it's best to take up watercolor painting then religious studies. Though spiritual studies compared to religious studies are far more educated. The study of spirituality is what all faiths has in common, but even that will only reap its poor rewards. It's only a poor reward for an ego-Mind's obsession with thinking it's as spiritual when it just has a big, deluded head!

One may think it odd that multiple units of the one exist in one domain, but so is true in the Sixth Dimension regarding multi-souls. Of the Six, the individual souls are unaware of each other; only their seventh-Dimensional overlord embodies them all as the perfections of so many souls. In the Eighth, one truly only has one Spirit, but is fragmented into multiple aspects of the self. The one Spirit alone and its numerous are like a hologram of the whole multiples given the one. It's much like a multi-headed and armed Hindu god/goddess-like Kali. According to my intuition alone, I feel that she is of the Eighth Dimension, as is Lord Krishna. These are very high abstract concepts. It is best to leave it to faith that this occurs. The domain of the Mind is our limits in terms of one's highest mental scope. A Jiva – one who evolves, has a subconscious ninth-dimensional awareness in all

Dimensions of multiverses with their many Realms all simultaneously embodying and including the Eighth but can only be fully aware of their own karmic path's destiny.

What is the directive of our current incarnation's spiritual evolution? The answer is abstract in that all rivers lead to the sea. Our rivers of unique individual karmic evolutionary paths are vast and only can be realized as one path of our Ninth Dimension Master Spirit. Our Master Spirit is both huge and very minuscule at the same time. In the chapter about the Ninth to the Twelve Dimensions, we shall discuss how one's many rivers of evolution in one means nothing but its ability to dismiss it all as if it never happened to begin. The Ninth doesn't recognize any of our egoic achievements. By the time our evolutionary path, of which we have many, reaches the Eighth as our many destinies. Our God theme has been seen as ridiculous by us in due time. Our Master Spirit usually encourages others to know God in different ways *themes* to be employed. The Master Spirit will stop using such *themes* only when their jokes are ridiculously repulsive; then, its consciousness is absorbed entirely in the next higher Dimension – the Ninth. We are currently trying to see through the riddle of knowing God better by trying to be Him. We will encounter numerous riddles pertaining to getting to know and understand God better along many lines of thought.

Our spirits are fractured in multiples to address any given riddle it is entertained within the Eight Dimension. A new spirit branch is given to answer a unique riddle it obliges to address. It reflects down to the First Dimension to organize itself politically with like-Minded souls. It then evolves upward in Dimension to reach the Ninth, where all riddles are resolved as ridiculous.

One thought adjuster is present at the eighth, but can cause more confusion than you think necessary—the thought adjuster chooses from numerous riddles to isolate down to around 10,000 riddles to address. If the many spirits are still lost in answering those riddles, the Lord of chaos is called to help them see how false those riddles are. It involves chaos down in those realities that the monad projects down. Our world's evil might be it assistance for us to see through our current riddle?

Lastly, the Mind is fully explained as being of matter and energy, but its true nature is indescribable and an element to itself. This nature, we can only relate to using yellow – Mind. Yellow is for joy, calms the nerves, is friendly, tunes our Minds, makes one laugh, and is fun! All these mentioned are needed in human life. It is not always the most practical or essential things in life that we need to strive for, but the simpler joys of life with friends can do much more for us. My closing advice on the Eighth Dimension is not to take life so seriously, but to enjoy every day as they come. Now, this is an eighth-Dimensional use of Mind – Joy!

Chapter 15

The Ninth to the Twelfth Dimensions Mulapakriti

Mulapakriti differs from the Mind in that consciousness is not used in the lower resolutions of the eighth-dimension themes of the Eighth Dimension. Mulapakriti is also the mother of both energy and matter but is detached from any evolutionary involvements. There is Mulapakriti in the Eight, but it's not oriented to answering those uncountably many Gods-related riddles not worth answering but nurtures instead. In the domain of the Master Spirit, the Ninth/Tenth Dimension, all riddles pertaining to knowing God better are beneath their status of the residing Master Spirit.

In the Ninth Dimension, we are in a negative polarity of Mulaprakiti, which makes the Master Spirit ever so receptive to the needs of its lower members in a nurturing manner. One might even think that the Master Spirit has a feminine gender like a goddess when the forces of the Eleventh Dimension have personas of a male god, with a Hemimorphite god in the Tenth Dimension. Though, over the Ninth, there is no notable manner of character. The Master Spirit's status is at the least seeming to have much of a personality above that, spirits are seen as forces of Nature with no central vortex of power or having much of a form of character.

These three forms of God proxies are instrumental in interventions and adjust from even higher Dimensions of God serving co-creators – Demigods. The three proxies are on their three levels of Mulapakriti – the Ninth, Tenth, and Eleventh Dimensions. The Demigods are there to make our bad dream here in the lower seven Dimensions as happy as possible. We are not aware how much work they do to bring happiness to our hearts – the three levels of Lords plus the twelfth-Dimensional psychiatrist Lords and even higher Lords – the Demigods are.

I will explain each level of Mulapakiti in full:

The Ninth Dimension: The Ninth is negatively charged and is the last place where the Spirit – consciousness, has character. Above the Ninth, spirits are void of personality will little self-consciousness. The Master Spirit's needs to have a light personality as their work involves downward applications to the souls of the lower Dimensions. In New Aged terms, our Master Spirit - *higher self* - needs to relate to us as a light character with a light personality to help us succeed.

This negatively charged Dimension of the Ninth needs such a charge to nurture and attract the lower eight Dimensions. The Ninth seems to reflect everything about the lower eight. The Master Spirits in the Ninth can only work with what is there. The Tenth Dimensional force can create any needed elements for the lower eight if required, like a genie. The Ninth Dimension also attracts dying Universes into itself. It does so: When dark energy and matter both out-balance Matter and energy in the outer reaches of a Universe, all four elements are inducted into the Ninth as negatively charged Mulapakriti. The forces from any of the lower seven dying Universe go to all three levels of Mulapakriti. Then they are balanced in the Tenth to be made manifest again in the Eleventh applied downward as a new big bang of new and differently created Universe, unlike any other, in any of the lower seven Dimensions.

The induction occurs in a Universe from the outer reaches in an induction sphere and waits until all matters and energies expand toward the induction zone's shell for total transformations. That is the end of Universal expansion. They are many false theories of how our Universe will end one will find. My intuitive abilities are sixty-seven percent accurate in this book. All good psychics are only on the same level of accuracy equal.

The Ninth is a mysterious field because it approves these ridiculous riddles by mistakenly trying to know God better in a vast array of different ways. The Ninth Dimension approves– Maya of the Eighth Dimension - in Tibetan to English - Illusion. Why does the Ninth approve of such oddly insane illusions? In numerology, the number Nine represents a spiritual awareness or revelation. In the dark, one must be unaware before one is truly awakened to what it is and is not. I have heard that the Buddha is an awaken principle. The true awakening is the initiation from the Ninth to the Tenth Dimensions.

A Master Spirit is a master in this initiation but, still cares to a server in the Ninth for lower souls out of love. The uninitiated are Sub Master Spirits who have lower selves in all lower Dimensions and multiverses and its many Realms to live out their Maya. They to help their lower members, but in a far more direct manner than – a Master Spirit can. Most Buddhist souls are of the Fifth Dimension where our original Buddha – in Sanskrit Siddhartha Gautama incarnated from to go to our planet in the sixth century B.C. The fact is, a Buddha is not truly awakened until he gets through the Ninth to the Tenth Dimension but still may serve on the Ninth as a Master Spirit. Not even Christ or Krishna is fully awakened. So, to become awakened, one must be asleep in the dreams of disillusionments first; this is what the Buddhist text called Maya – entanglement in the matter and identifying with the soul/body. The soul is just an interface with the unknown. The souls are created out of a misunderstanding of the Spirit. The body is just the soul's lower vehicle in lower domains/realities.

The Tenth Dimension: The Tenth is neutrally charged at balancing the Ninth's negative and Eleventh positive charges. The Tenth Dimension is where new Universes are logistically arranged according to unique math algorithms reflecting the First and Second Dimensions as a ground.

The math needed for new Universes must stem from the First but to be worked out my second Dimensional high mathematical lords before they manifest from the Eleventh Dimension to anywhere in the lower seven Dimensions. The First Dimensional Lords work hand-to-hand with the Eight Dimensions Lords in ringing forward a new ridiculous God name/riddle in knowing Him better. However, the Ninth-Dimensional forces must approve these riddles as needed for one's experience. The tenth dimensional lord finally gives the real explanation as to why these riddles are all false individually.

The Tenth Dimension is the place where one gets complete, terminates an old cycle, and is on a new upwards. This domain is the first place where one is initiated as a son of God and who knows God. The initiated lord's status had resolved all ridiculous riddles to be worked out in the Tenth. One is at the center of their being and master of their reality. They are the one and zero to make the ten - the one conscious Spirit with the touching reach of God. True God-awareness isn't until the Thirteenth Dimension, though, where one loses their self-consciousness totally to the universal subconsciousness of God.

The Eleventh Dimension: This Dimension is positively charged and is where the Universal strings to all substances originate. These strings are devices in the Tenth but made manifest in the Eleventh. All lower substances are commanded from this Dimensions force of creativity. All of creation is made manifest there in the Eleventh by its lords.

They are the one and the one to make the eleven. We have then the individual of yet a higher individual here in the eleven. One has started its path to higher planes of Life as a God be known Spirit to work out its own will. Note I said – will? One still has self-will in the Eleventh.

Only can a godly will be seen in the Thirty-first Dimension. The Spirit here still has self-will and consciousness but is under direction by higher demigods. One has a sense of a godlike government in their consciousness, but still how the Spirit deems such messages to be. The Spirit interprets according to its self-will God's plan for our happiness in all our creations.

The twelfth Dimension: This Dimension is the completion of all the creations of all ages beyond God's plans for all of us. I say rejoice because these self-deluded plans are not of God's Mind and logic. There are far too many so-called – *plans for salvation.* The only regard God has for them in the way of a blessing is if we all seem to rely on these plans for salvation, God will try to make them work. Will they work? Only enough to fool us. God's blessing of them entails us to see through them all. The Twelfth Dimension is not Mulapakriti but far away from any creative forces. The Lords, there maintain safe objectivity to us to help us do our best. The environment used far less mathematically insane logic as the lower one does. The only negative aspect of this domain is that it tried to perfect all aspects of Life beyond any limits. This fault impedes its appropriate counseling and may further foster Maya. The initiation out of that Dimension entails accepting Life for what it is apart from what we feel it should be. The topic of Life itself is taken up in the Twelfth Dimension.

One can reach out to other spirits in a cooperative venture in understanding the creations of the insane lower Mind. The twelfth-Dimensional lords only work as advisors and physiologists to aid lower life forms to sanity. They are not creative lords- Demiurge, but spiritual physiologists to assist those self-destructive to sanity and happiness. We start seeing Demigod/Demiurges in higher realities. In this Dimension, true spirituality is first seen. If there might be a true religion, it's in the twelfth Dimension. The twelfth dimensional lords oversee all religions everywhere to know that they function as they should. Here on our planet, we feel spirituality is a study of God when the goal should be obtaining true sanity. God is God; He does not need adorations. We, the sick here, need such self-love to regain our true sense. God is sane. We are not! If we unselfishly love ourselves – that is loving God!

Chapter 16

13th to 33rd Dimensions Co-creators with God – Demigods

We may now be able to see through this whole system we agreed upon in its entrance and its departure. The question about One to Thirty-Three Dimension is a curiosity. Why thirty-three Dimensions? The answer rest in our numerology. Our system of numerology is from zero to thirty-three. 33 is a master number like 22, and 11 are. There are 33 vertebrates in our spinal cord; there are 32 plus 1 initiation of the Free Mansions. Our system of One to Thirty-Three Dimension is local and sympathetic to the numerology we use is not true. The ranges used in this dimensional system are relative to the numerology systems. They are used to reflect another standard used in life to confirm its numerological value. A whole Universe may have various ranges of numbers Dimensions applied. In these respects, the entire system of evolution seems wild and unregulated!

This group of Dimension of the teens is still holding to personal self-will. The higher Lords of the twenties – Demigods allow these lower Demigods to assist in the souls lost in creation – *the dimensional life in the Universes and Realms under the Eighth Dimension*. The higher Lords allow the lower lords of this group to use their free will's even if they may make mistakes or decisions that are not very productive. The rule is that this group of lower lords adds those in creation; however, when things are severely counterproductive, the higher lords of the twenties step in to adjust manners. All ruling forces are from the Ninth Dimension, though higher lords can influence the consciousness of the ninth's Dimensional lords outside of their awareness. The considerations of the lords in the teens and twenties apply to *psychologists like Lords* in the Ninth to condition the Ninth Lords consciousness to correct counsel to lower lives under them.

Yes, both sets of Lords of the teens and the twenties have unique creative works beyond what we call – creation. They are more so in tune with the true logic of God and how He would have His sons co-create with Him. In the teens, they seem to use their wills to co-create, which does not always reflect the divinity of God. For that fact, our whole system of Thirty- three Dimensions was most surely devices by such lower Demigod lords.

The thirteens dimensional lords have united with God's logic and have lost their rebellious self-consciousness. The very thought of self-consciousness must insist that God is dead, and the self is the only ruling Lord. Upon losing one's self-consciousness, they openly accept God as their father and source of all life. Not even the Pope in Rome, The Dali Lama, can say that they have accepted God as their source of life. One may say so, but in our life status, we are fooling ourselves if we state that same affirmation. Yes, one still has self-will in the Dimensions of the teen. The difference between self-consciousness and self-will is seen as apples to oranges to tangerines to oranges. Self-consciousness and self-will are two different things. Having self-will does not require God to be dead, but God's laws of self-interpret freely.

Self-will relies on one own understanding, in these lords' cases, of an interpretation of God's logic to their understandings while still accepting God as their source. They are accepting God as our source means allowing God to live in our lives. Doing so indicates to us as reflecting His sanity and logic. It is fine enough to interpret His will in the teen's Dimensions to work out one delusion of God's logic and sanity; this is a needed field of exercise for higher life forms to work out.

Dimensions 14 to 19 are explained as: My God will be done.

The fourteenth dimensional Lord's works with a more mathematically constructive proven form of logic from experience. The Fifteen's Dimensional lords work more so with the magic of the Divine using faith in God's wonders to co-create. The sixteenth-dimensional lords feel responsibilities, in a family way, using the lust of life itself to bless all and create using Divine lust. This lust involves other lord corporations but still struggling to use one will. The fight of will here is between *the lords* and its *prodigies* that are beyond them to surrender their logic to God's logic in a deeper faith requiring manner. The seventeenth-dimensional lords use God's logic far more by seeing their free will as possibly ungodly and crating beyond their self-limitations. The eighteenth-dimensional lords use their own personal powers of infinity to create and advise lower lords. Infinity is an eternal divine force; it is a void in life that deals with the true reality of life everywhere. The nineteenth-dimensional lords are seeking marriage with other lords. They do so to kill their free will and be reborn into a more cooperative group of the Dimension of the twenty's co-creators.

Dimensions 20 to 29 are explained as - The end of free will.

This group of Dimensions host Demigod lords who are true co-creators with God using His logic totally. No more the - *My will be done as I seem to understand God's logic,* but a far humbler way of being as not relying on one's understandings. One no longer relies on their understanding of God's logic. These lords use His logic freely and cooperate with other Demigods, Lord, in a group effort. They seem to marry us by marriage and reborn marriage unions of the Nineteenth Dimension or in the Lord.

The lords of the Twentieth Dimension are two and zero to make twenties. The divine marriage of God, like a nun, marriages Jesus and serves a lifelong commitment. One is committed to God's laws and logic as His way of living. One does have creations and gives aid to the lower Master Spirits as needed. Even though our whole system of creation was devices by self-willed Demigods, the higher lords of the twenties bless their logic to make the whole system function joyously and happily. Their main concern is for souls to be able to freely leave their entrapments and reunite to God's sanity at any given point. The entrance and departure of souls and spirits in and out to create a quasi-sense of divinity in the whole growth system of our many Dimensions. The lords of the Twenty-first are vigilant in doing God's will alone and are the most active in this group of the twenties. The lords of the Twenty-second are only concerned with group inter-reactions being of God's higher love and sanity. The lords of the Twenty- third are producers of many new creations unknowns before enforcing the infinity of God further; creations use joy as their power. A joy is an unknown power to humanity currently.

We have not tapped into the true powers of Joy yet. The lords of the Twenty-fourth are lords of manifestations of creation in union with God's sane logic. Their creations are unknown to us here on Earth and are beyond our scope of Mind. The lords of the Twenty-fifth are a wizard in creating new realities that might even surprise God. Their logic is godly and brings out logically unknown creation using the magic of the power of God Himself. God's true influences are first felt in the Twenty-Fifth Dimensions. The lords of the Twenty-sixth are in love and union with their source – God. All co-creations are a prodigy of such love. The truly Divine is first felt there. The lords of the Twenty-seventh are starting to question if they are not in true union with God. They created divine art and beauty out of their self-questioning of their doubted marriages. The lords of the Twenty-eighth are going into the void of God for the first time. The void or being all things and nothing at the same time. The lords of the Twenty-ninth are the divorce of false unions with Demi-god and the true marriage of God Himself.

The life forms of the Thirties are not Demi-gods, but faceless creative forces to be used by God most passively. The Thirty-first Dimension is a true God force made real. Thirty-two is this God force being used in a cooperative. Thirty-three is nonbeing but being in a void of no definition or understandings. They are genuinely faceless, with no use, no description, but truly of God's love and joy. Out of such love and joy, all powers are giving them. One just needs to be at peace with God outside of any actions or trying to be anything but too simple - Be. The Lords of the thirties are likened to the Qabalah Ain Soph Aur or *the living light with to beginning or end*. The only personality akin to the 33rd is the high Lord Metatron. He is the voice of God. One can never address him face to face but request his help through the angel Gabriel, Michael, Urial, or Raphael.

I end this chapter with a quote from Edgar Cayce of A.R.E - Association of Research and enlightenment

"Be still and know that you are at one with God"

Chapter 17

Dimension of the beyond The Fire of God

According to my intuition and online findings, the Forty-second Dimension is the perfect Dimension mathematically. All Dimensions before and after will be less perfect mathematically. The high demi-gods of the Twenties had to anchor the whole dimensional system of One to One hundred-twenty-three as its axis in the Forty-second Dimension. The limits and the perfect Dimension rest are all relative to the culture of the planetary system where the souls live. I am only indicating our relative facts of life in our planet Earth's system of related higher Dimensions.

After the Forty-second, Dimension is less perfect and less able to host any living forces. The life forces that inhabit those oddly discolored Dimensions are advanced life forces that enjoy a *freer reign of life* with less mathematical interferences. These imperfect Dimensions are more perfect for the higher powers to apply a more counter-logistical way to be, which is the definition of reality unknown to us currently. The logic reflecting Earth and the logic reflecting advanced life forces manifest in two different ways. This hither Dimension can be less perfect for us, but more perfect to the higher progressive forces of life.

The life forces are there to moderate the whole system of 123 Dimensions with Dimension Forty-two as its axis. The demi-gods of the Twenties need such an axis with moderations from the hither Dimensions life forces for proper orientations in decision-making and their creation in their realities. The demi-gods in the twenties hold the math needed to muscle all that is. From what I can hear, the efforts required seem to go against their higher logic and abilities. Did we hear of the strong angels of God? They are there in their twenties to regulate and adjust all life. The faceless powers of the thirties give them the power needed to do their great works. Those Strong Angels need to incarnate to lower realities to check in with them for their overall attunements. When they do come down, they are usually quite gorgeous and strong. They keep out of sight, but are seen enough and worship others for their beauty. Both May West and Gloria Swanson were two of these high Lords from the dimensions of the twenties to reorient their essence of life to help us better.

One thing we have not considered is a life far outside of any Earthly wild reflected Dimensions. Yes, that is where the true and perfect sanity of the logic of God rests. It is beyond my means to describe such life and environments relating to its perfections. The best I can indicate is from our Thirty-third Dimension; how all is made manifest in being still and secure with no needs or wants – just supreme peace and security. It is called – The Void! It can be experienced in the Thirty-third, but in a representative manner only. The real Void is experienced far outside of any use of math. All 231Dimensions use math to a larger or lesser extent.

The True Void is Divinity without any descriptions are word to say about it – it purely is the Void. We might find it hard to accept that imperfect lords in the dimensions of the teens have devised the reality we live in. Their works would not have functions and be made suitable for life if not for even higher Demi-gods to adjust their logic to a quasi-perfect level. Quasi-perfect is the best blessing the higher lords can offer us. The vehicle for God's Holy Spirit is found in the dimensions of the thirties as its home base.

Cannot be applied truly perfect logic in our realities as it will destroy it. God's logic is like a *devastating fire* that will destroy all life, this Fire of true life. We cannot get too near to this Fire but stand outside of and remain in a convoluted use of math to make our realities. The logic of this Fire cannot be described, but to say that it's the opposite of what we find here in our grand system or life might be a start in the true understanding of God. This Fire stands at the edges of the 123-dimensional system. One would need to die in our reality by being purged by the pure, godly Fire and be reborn to one's perfections with God in the true Void of eternal peace and security to experience true life. In the Zoroastrian faith, God is seen as the Fire of wisdom. In a Zoroastrian temple, a central eternal flame is never put out, but remains lite like the temple of the Vestal Virgins of ancient Rome.

Chapter 18

Our Third/Fourth-Dimensional growth and destiny

I t is a rarely written topic concerning the fourth-dimensional polarity we have on our Planet Earth. It does not happen very much in our Universe at all. This polarity offers a downward flood of fourth-dimensional attunements to our living standards; this comes from the polarity shift and having many interventions in our reality from fourth-dimensional souls there.

The souls who live in the Fourth Dimension are very compassionate and loving. They know precisely how one feels on all matters and are very sensitive to maintaining harmony in their interactions with others. Having a good rapport in their speech is unavoidable as any disharmonies only torment the lesser one involved. They live in a peaceful environment and are called Nirvana by the Hindu faith. In Sanskrit, the word Nirvana means *the quench of one's soul*: referring to human passions and desires in life. Life in the Fourth is far less ego-driven and materialistic compared to us. They are happier in this way.

Such advanced life is at our doorsteps to attune us to their level of excellence. We experience their influences in our world's religions and societies. Such advanced souls from Nirvana directly influenced our United Nations Organization in New York City; our whole religious-based governing of peoples is under their influences. Those advanced souls incarnated to our Planet Earth to install these institutions initiated the practice of diplomacy. Many incarnates from the Fourth have set a higher standard for us to speed up our progress here on Earth. Our Earth mother – Gaia, insisted upon their service and attunements to their standards so we here on Earth now can evolve and to move onward to a higher life - and to leave her alone.

We will leave Earth when it gets too hot. However, Gaia will soon enough lower the carbon dioxide to cool the planet down for the growth of animal and plant life for quite a few million years before it gets hot once more for the last time. The high counsel of Nirvana – a group of fourth dimension star system culture -approved of this plan two hundred and thirty thousand Earth years ago with the development of the Neanderthals with further developments in 28,000 BCE. with modern man. However, in 195,000 BCE, Homo sapiens migrated out of Africa to Europe and Asia, then over the world. In the year 50,000 BCE, the man started to farm and raise livestock first. These developments were overseen by many foreign cultures – the Elohim/ Anunnaki, Gaia herself, and the fourth and seventh-dimensional hierarchies.

Both the Hindu and Buddhist faiths were encouraged by this Dimension. The hierarchy of these fourth-dimensional cultures sought out advanced souls to plant those faiths on Earth. The Buddha of the Fifth Dimension and Lord Krishna of the Eighth Dimension was found and employed to our planet. First Lord Krishna in 17/18 June 3229 BCE, and the Buddha is 640 BCE. The Tao was written in 2500 BCE by Lao Tzu with I Ching in the year 1000 BCE. The Christ consciousness was established in the year 132 A.D by a Roman named - Flavius Justinus. Flavius was the first Christian philosopher to summarize Christian beliefs into one concise manner of teachings with one central theme. His teachings were the first organized argument to establish this Christ consciousness. Before he was many views on Christ with no central theme or idea – they were just scattered statements of Jesus and the written works of Yosef Mathias – Josephus.

The Hierarchy of the Fourth Dimension inspired the original written work by Mohamad's 144 poems in 570 - 622 AD, and both the

Christian Science and Theosophy in the mid-1800s were implanted by their hierarchical souls. Not just religion, but good governments, art, drama, music, and higher studies of math and architecture. Yes. We have our Dharma – duties to be – and there is confusion between the two. The only way to mix the two is to be of our higher inspiration in our ego-driven manner. The world religions are full of ego like any other inspired study I mentioned. So, we need to see the marriage between the two.

How this works out in our everyday life is to have far more harmonious relationships with real conversation holding a true rapport and agreements. Inter - reaction of advanced life in other star system's culture is not very personal – but impersonal with little to say for emotions or rapports. The higher life forms have peace in their worlds, but aliens do not associate and chat as we do and enjoy each other's company. They find that conversations are not very fruitful, but a waste of time; they do not see the unifying emotional aspect for their higher growths as we do. I have mentioned before that advanced alien races are jealous of our fast existing into the Fourth Dimension. At the same time, they will be left behind in our Third Dimension to evolve and learn these qualities more slowly over numerous incarnations and worlds of growth. Even though our Dharma is not directly third dimensional and confusing at times, we will grow faster and be in the Nirvana way before other – so-called – advanced life in the Third Dimension.

Chapter 19

What is meant by one's return to God?

The return to God is a regaining of one's sanity apart from any devices using a pseudo-reality designed using math as its basis of functioning. One would need to know why they left God's sanity first to regain that sanity. To understand this would have to go into split characters' psychology. The fact remains that we never left God's side to be insane in such a pseudo-reality. The moment we fell into it, the correction was made for the restoration of our sanity. Time does not exist with God, so that no time can measure its healing. What time is, is a shock reaction to a bad thought of questioning God's love for us applied to the (analysis – *time*) of what this thought was. *Time* was invented to analyze such a wrong thought. They say time is an *illusion*. What they mean is that *time* is created out of fear. In God's eyes, fear does not exist; it never did and never will exist.

We have time in the Second to the Seventh Dimensions to a lesser degree as one gets higher in those Dimensions. All higher Dimensions are auxiliary and at service to the lower six Dimensions. This shock is felt up to the 123rd Dimension but understood perfectly in the Forty-second Dimension. The key for our release and return to God is in the Forty - Second Dimension, where such a wrong thought is truly questioned in counter to its reality itself. The truth is seen using God's Fire, which opens one up to true logic and sanity.

The riddle of our whole pseudo-reality is one riddle. The infinite riddle of the Eighth Dimensional sets are sub-riddles to the main one. The answer to the central riddle is different to each son of God here in our pseudo-reality of many mathematically designed Dimensions.

That central riddle, maybe – can we have God love us more and we Him more? The demi-gods of the Dimension from Fourteen and higher know the answer to this riddle, but are here to assist us in our return to sanity when we are ready to encounter the Divine Fire of God. They are to Bodhisattva who remain with all lost ones until the last son of God is at one with their sanity with God.

The higher lords of the Twenties had infused rescuing ways for us to exit this pseudo-reality resulting in a blink of an eye, one is back to their sanity with God. The Divine Fire of God is used in this way. One pass through this Fire to burn away any impurities to their nature. A Greek myth tells the same story of Demeter, who fed her child Danophone ambrosia during the day then put him in the Fire at night to burn away his mortality. The ambrosia is divine knowledge and the Fire of God's purifying nature.

I wrote that we never left God's side, and our stay in this pseudo-reality is a projection dream we are experiencing. So, the question remains: If we never left God's side and this is just a projection, is the projection purified or what is? I respond by saying, when one is in shock, they act as if their whole being is in that reaction. Even though by God's side, in His Divine true reality, the illusion needs to be treated and not denied as if its reality is whole-bodied. No matter where in the lower Dimensions one may be, the Thirteenth Dimension's loss of consciousness stage is required for one's recovery. From there, in timelessness, the Dimensions of the Teens and Twenties may pass in a twinkle of an eye, then one's union with God is made. In timelessness, one can evolve through many realities of trillions of Earth years but be as a twinkle of an eye to the son of God to his actual state.

Referring to the healing process for those who return directly to God's sanity, I say that the Divine Fire is a volunteer and needed self-love to accept the wrong thought of God and to open one's to Divine love. Yes, even at the right-hand side of God, one still needs to instill the true and Divinity of God's love. True - Heaven is perfect, but that does not mean that it cannot be questioned. The questioning of God's love for us does cause such a projection into these pseudo-realities of these bad dreams. We have these bad dreams because we try to love God more and, in return, Him loving us more. In a Muslim myth of Lucifer and God, Lucifer felt that humanity did not love God enough, so he caused chaos for humanity to appreciate God's love more by rescuing them from such chaos. We might have put God to the test by coming here to our shaded realities to see if God will save us as well.

So, does God rescue us? We are the author of our bad dream, and we must come of sanity in our own due time. God can only bless our Sense Memory of who He is. The Catholic faith called this Sense Memory – God's Holy Spirit. If God was to be accredited in helping us return to sanity, all He did was blessed this Memory to aid and guarantee our return. Such Sense Memory also enables all higher dimensional servants to rescue us, to God's love, and try to make this bad dream as happy as possible out of God's loving nature. Yes, God goes along with our joke of depicting His nature as an affectionate portrait; we paint Him here out of love and acceptance of anything we do. Still, sanity is sanity, and when we have had enough fun here, it's time to return to God like Godchildren returning from their play.

Our numerous secondary riddles of the Eighth Dimension are secondary to our Grand Riddle that caused our original and whole separation into this pseudo-reality is: *Can we love God more, in turn, God love us more?*

Life in God's love is open to questions through His God-giving free will He gives to us. Regardless of that, the reality is always retained in a timeless healing moment back to sanity.

The answer to life's Grand Riddle is – No! We cannot love God more and his love for us more in return. I can intellectually and poetically write this – but to be ready for its acknowledgment is personally and prepared in one due time.

Conclusion

I close this book by quoting the *eighth-dimensional riddle* of – *knowing God by trying to be Him,* our *Grand Riddle of striving to love God more to get more love back.* Both riddles will be resolved in due time or at a given moment in time in a twinkle of an eye; we will be back to our sanity with God. All that is asked of us currently is to experience a radiating joy that touches all equally and follows our bliss in life. Try to make this bad dream into a good dream. Try to deserve love with the right partner and friends. We have our Sense Memory of God – the Holy *Spirit* to turn over all our unhappiness to help us. We will see in life's reflections the answers and the healing of our sadness.

In our current Third/Fourth Dimension, the best we can be recognized as a good person of virtue with fine rapport with others. It is fine to have that expensive car and house with fashionable clothes in our Dimension. We are in the world to be seen and adored. It is fine to have that special loved one who loves us exclusively; It is fine to deserve true love here. Our fourth-dimensional polarity influences us to do all the above elegantly. The Dali Lama said: *If we can be all nice to each other, mostly all world evil will fade away.* This statement is a Nirvana-influenced thought. We must try to be as spiritual and charitable as possible here for our best growth. We must try to manifest God as a man or a woman to its full here in the Third Dimension. Get out and be a movie star or a stage actor, a rich man or woman, or a big, famous politician. Lovingly do all these things or be who we are now if that pleases us. Do not be an audience member, be on the grand screen. We are stars in our own right!

Yes, spiritual evolution is a joke, but most are subjected to it because of self-hatred from a deluded notion that we had to kill God to obtain our self-consciousness. The very thought of having self-consciousness is rebellion in Heaven. The story about the fallen angels refers to our need for a self-consciousness. The archangel Michael works as a psychiatrist to help us loosen that psychological ailment; it is acceptable to pray to him. The main reason why we need self-consciousness is to analyze how insane our two riddles are. Insanity can only breed further insanity, which we call life here in our insane and sometimes evil world.

At any spit second, one can be transported back to our normal state of sanity with God. But getting it straight and truly knowing our sense of God is a normal attitude is beyond most people if they are not mystic nuns or priests from years past. The study of esoteric saints is better after reading this book we are finishing now and the only material I can recommend from our standpoint. Not to mention my first book - The enigma of God, a revelation to man.

This book, above all, it's considered to be *Mysticism* due to its automatic writings used to write this book – *Personal growth in the multi-dimensional multiverse.*

I thank you all for your support.

Author Frank Marcello Antonetti
– New Orleans la in November of 2021

Biography

I was born and grew up in the metropolitan area of New Jersey/New York City. I tried a few religions but felt out of place. After the Army in 1986 at age 27, I moved to New York City and worked as a phone reservationist for an Airline – Virgin. I learned alternative spirituality in New York and later Theosophy at the United Lodge of Theosophy. Christian Science is my prayer technique along with Wiccan devotions and rituals. I published my first book – The enigma of God, a revelation to man - in 2012 with Balboa press while living in NYC. I lived in Miami Beach of seven years and now in New Orleans to write my current book. I find that magic is much stronger here in New Orleans and the Jazz to be fabulous. I plan to move back to South Florida in a few years and write a third book which will be a help-help book on *Virtues and Vices*.

Thank you,
Frank Marcello Antonetti

Printed in the United States
by Baker & Taylor Publisher Services